Just Marriage

EDITED BY
Joshua Cohen and Deborah Chasman
for *Boston Review*

Other books in the
NEW DEMOCRACY FORUM / BOSTON REVIEW series

Mary Lyndon Shanley

Just Marriage

OXFORD
UNIVERSITY PRESS

2004

OXFORD
UNIVERSITY PRESS

Oxford   New York
Auckland   Bangkok   Buenos Aires   Cape Town   Chennai
Dar es Salaam   Delhi   Hong Kong   Istanbul   Karachi   Kolkata
Kuala Lumpur   Madrid   Melbourne   Mexico City   Mumbai   Nairobi
São Paulo   Shanghai   Taipei   Tokyo   Toronto

Copyright © 2004 by *Boston Review*

Published by Oxford University Press, Inc.
198 Madison Avenue, New York, New York 10016

www.oup.com

Oxford is a registered trademark of Oxford University Press

Library of Congress Cataloging-in-Publication Data
Shanley, Mary Lyndon, 1944–
Just marriage / by Mary Lyndon Shanley ; edited by Joshua Cohen
and Deborah Chasman for Boston Review
    p. cm.
ISBN 0-19-517625-1; 0-19-517626-X (pbk.)
1. Marriage—United States. 2. Marriage—Government policy—United States.
I. Cohen, Joshua, 1951– II. Chasman, Deborah. III. Title.
HQ536.S4815 2004
306.81'0973—dc22   2004006517

9 8 7 6 5 4 3 2 1

Printed in the United States of America
on acid-free paper

In memory of Susan Moller Okin

Contents

Contributors

Wendy Brown is Professor of Political Science and Women's Studies at the University of California, Berkeley, and author of *Edgework: Essays on Knowledge and Politics*.

Drucilla Cornell is Professor of Political Science, Women's Studies, and Comparative Literature at Rutgers University and author of *Beyond Accommodation* and *The Imaginary Domain*.

Brenda Cossman is Professor of Law at the University of Toronto and Visiting Professor at Harvard Law School. She is coeditor of *Privatization, Law, and the Challenge to Feminism*.

Nancy F. Cott is Jonathan Trumbull Professor of American History at Harvard University. Her most recent book is *Public Vows: A History of Marriage and the Nation*.

David B. Cruz is Professor of Law at the University of Southern California Law School.

Elizabeth F. Emens is Bigelow Teaching Fellow and Lecturer in Law at the University of Chicago Law School.

William N. Eskridge Jr. is John A. Garver Professor of Jurisprudence at Yale Law School and author of *The Case for Same-Sex Marriage* and *Equality Practice: Civil Unions and the Future of Gay Rights*.

Amitai Etzioni is a University Professor at George Washington University, founder and first president of the Communitarian Network, and author most recently of *My Brother's Keeper: A Memoir and a Message*.

Martha Albertson Fineman is Robert W. Woodruff Professor of Law at Emory Law School and author of *The Autonomy Myth* and *The Neutered Mother, the Sexual Family, and Other Twentieth Century Tragedies*.

Tamara Metz is a doctoral candidate in the government department at Harvard University.

Milton C. Regan Jr. is Professor of Law at the Georgetown University Law Center and author of *Alone Together: Law and the Meanings of Marriage* and *Family Law and the Pursuit of Intimacy*.

Mary Lyndon Shanley is Margaret Stiles Halleck Professor of Political Science at Vassar College. Her most recent book is *Making Babies, Making Families*.

Cass R. Sunstein is Karl N. Llewellyn Distinguished Service Professor, University of Chicago Law School and Department of Political Science, and author of *The Second Bill of Rights*, *Why Societies Need Dissent*, and *Designing Democracy*.

Joan C. Tronto is Professor of Political Science and Women's Studies at Hunter College and the Graduate Center, City University of New York, and author of *Moral Boundaries: A Political Argument for an Ethic of Care*.

I

Mary Lyndon Shanley

Just Marriage
On the Public Importance of Private Unions

American conservatives pride themselves on moral clarity. And that clarity is nowhere greater than on the topic
of marriage and family. The essentials of marriage are, they
say, well defined: it unites a man and a woman; it provides the
foundation for a family that may include biological or adopted
children; it assigns different roles to men and women; and it
is a union for life, indissoluble except for the most grievous
offenses. These essentials are, according to conservatives, not
a product of the vagaries of social convention or contingent
cultural choices but are instead given by nature, scripture,
or tradition. Moreover, preserving them is intrinsically good
for individuals and has great public benefits: marriage is the

foundation of society, and a strong foundation will protect against society's ills, from crime to poverty.

For the past decade conservatives have worked energetically to implement this vision—more precisely, to restore it in the face of the demographic, economic, and cultural changes of the past forty years. They have defended the two-parent marriage by requiring (in the 1996 Welfare Reform Act) that single parents who receive welfare work outside the home for wages, while allowing one parent in a two-parent family that receives welfare to stay home to take care of the children. They have supported President George W. Bush's "marriage initiative," which allocates federal funds to programs intended to persuade unwed parents to marry—by rewarding, for example, a single mother who marries her child's father. And they have opposed efforts to legalize same-sex marriage in individual states and praised the federal Defense of Marriage Act, which exempts states from recognizing same-sex marriages entered into in other states. The Catholic bishops of Massachusetts, for example, have recently been pressing the state legislature to pass a constitutional amendment against same-sex marriage: such marriages will, they say, have "devastating consequences." And Ken Connor, then the president of the conservative Family Research Council, promised in 2003 to make a "big, big issue in 2004" out of the idea that "marriage [is] a sacred covenant, limited to a man and a woman."

Critics argue that these efforts to shore up the traditional family represent an assault on thirty years of sensible reforms of marriage and divorce law that have helped to free women and men from stultifying or abusive relationships; that they threaten to reimpose oppressive gender roles; that they stigmatize and disadvantage unwed mothers and their children; and that they condemn gay men and lesbians to second-class citizenship. In short, the conservative program is characterized as an enemy of equality and a threat to personal liberty.

But these critics have been less clear about their own constructive moral and political vision. One response to the conservative project has been to concentrate on efforts to legalize gay and lesbian marriage by reforming state marriage laws. This strategy is attractive and shows some promise in a few states, but even if it succeeds it leaves other elements of the conservative project untouched. It does nothing to address the concerns of those who regard marriage itself as oppressive, to remedy the poverty that deters some people from marrying, or to support single parents and their children.

A second, more comprehensive proposal—put forward by, among others, Lenore Weitzman in *The Marriage Contract* and Martha Fineman in *The Neutered Mother*—is to abolish state-defined marriage altogether and replace it with individual contracts drawn up by each couple wishing to marry. A regime of individual contracts would allow spouses to decide for themselves how to arrange their lives, and it would enable people of the same sex, or more than two persons, to marry. According to this view, which I will call contractualism, the best way to treat citizens as free and equal adults is to stop affording marriage a special public status and permit the parties themselves to define its terms and conditions.

Contractualism has considerable force, but it suffers from two deficiencies. First, the contract model treats persons as rational and bounded individuals while paying insufficient attention to the mutual need and dependence that arise in marriage and other close relationships. It thus rests on an incomplete view of the person and fails to take into account the ideal of marriage as a relationship that transcends the individual lives of the partners. That ideal has deep cultural resonance, and contractualism unnecessarily concedes this ground to conservatives. Second, while emphasizing the need for liberty in the choice of partners, contractualism fails to give sufficient weight to positive state action to enhance equality and equal opportunity along with liberty and freedom of association. It is thus founded on too narrow a conception of justice.

A third line of response, then, would preserve the idea that a married couple is something more than its separate members, and that spouses can make claims in the name of their relationship that are not identical to claims that each could make as individuals. But it would also open up marriage so that both women and men, regardless of race, class, or sexual orientation, could, as equals, assume the responsibilities and reap the rewards of family life. I will call this the equal status view. Its defining aspiration is to preserve the idea that marriage is a special bond deserving of a public status while rejecting—as incompatible with liberty and equality—important elements of the traditional view of the purpose and proper ordering of marriage.

Can marriage be reformed to serve as a public institution that promotes equality and liberty? Is the happy combination of justice, committed intimacy, and love suggested by the equal status view a real possibility?

I. From Fixed Status to No-Fault

The traditional view of marriage in the United States has roots in Christian religious views and church law. English common law, which provided the basis for the marriage laws of most states, reflected the tenets of marriage promulgated by the Anglican (and before it the Catholic) Church. When jurisdiction over marriage and children was transferred from the Church to common-law courts, public law for the most part simply took over aspects of Church doctrine.[1]

The Traditional View

In the Church's view, marriage was first and foremost a covenant, like God's covenant with the Jews and Christ's covenant with the church (the community of the faithful). Christian marriage was thus an unbreakable bond (for Catholics, a sacrament). Marriage was to be lifelong, and marital faithfulness was to include monogamy.

Marriage was also regarded as a hierarchical relationship in which husband and wife played complementary roles. The man was given authority as head of household. Blackstone, the eighteenth-century legal authority, explained that since Genesis declared husband and wife to be "one flesh" in the eyes of God, they were to be "one person" in the eyes of the law, and that person was represented by the husband. This suspension of the wife's legal personality was known as the doctrine of spousal unity or "coverture." Under coverture a married woman could not sue or be sued unless her husband was party to the suit, could not sign contracts unless he joined her, and could not make a valid will unless he consented to its provisions. As a correlate to these powers and his role as head of the family, a husband was obligated to support his wife and children. And since he would be held responsible for her actions, a husband had a right to correct his wife physically and to determine how and where their children would be raised. As late as 1945 a New Jersey court wrote:

> The plaintiff [husband] is the master of his household. He is the managing head, with control and power to preserve the family relation, to protect its members and to guide their conduct. He has the obligation and responsibility of supporting, maintaining and protecting the family and the correlative right to exclude intruders and unwanted visitors from the home despite the whims of the wife.[2]

Marriage was to be a structure in which the roles of the spouses were distinct and complementary: the wage earner and the housewife, the protector and the protected, the independent and the dependent.

The husband was expected to govern his household with neither interference nor help from the state. For the most part, the police turned a blind eye to violence between spouses. In most jurisdictions wives could not prosecute their husbands for marital rape because the law assumed that by marrying, spouses gave blanket consent to sexual relations (they were, after all, "one body" and "one person" in law). And judges enforced obligations of support only if spouses separated or divorced, not in ongoing marriages.

When people married, then, they entered a relationship whose terms were set by the state. Of course, the consent of the partners was a necessary precondition, but the agreement to marry brought with it rights and duties that were not set by the partners but were treated as intrinsic to the institution of marriage.

The First Wave of Reform

The unequal provisions of marriage law became the object of reform efforts in the mid–nineteenth century. Reformers were critical, for example, of the fact that many states granted divorce only for a wife's adultery and not a husband's. Moreover, adultery was in many states the only grounds for divorce, and some men and women began to insist that other wrongs, particularly physical cruelty and domestic violence, were significant offenses against the marriage that justified dissolving the marital bond. To forbid divorce in such instances, they said, was to make the home a "prison" for unhappy and wronged spouses, depriving them of essential personal liberty.

Feminist reformers also challenged coverture by invoking the principle of equality. They organized campaigns in a series of states to pass laws that would allow wives to hold property, sue and be sued, and enter contracts in their own names. By the end of the nineteenth century, many states had passed married women's property statutes, freeing married women from many of the legal effects of coverture.

While this first wave of marriage-law reform increased both the freedom to leave unsatisfactory marriages and equality between husbands and wives, dissatisfaction with marriage law remained. The grounds for divorce remained restrictive: several states still granted divorce only for adultery. And the law continued to treat married men and women differently: for example, many states imposed alimony only on husbands, a stipulation that assumed, and perhaps helped to perpetuate, women's exclusion from the paid labor force. The age at which females could marry without their parents' consent was often younger than that for males, suggesting that boys needed to stay in school or learn a trade before marrying and that girls did not. Custody laws varied widely but often contained a preference for mother's custody, again assuming that the mother was and would in the future be the better caregiver.

The Second Wave of Reform

In the mid–twentieth century a variety of factors (which I can only briefly allude to here) converged to spark a second wave of marriage-law reform. Demographic changes after 1900 were dramatic. Life expectancy for women was fifty-one years in 1900 and seventy-four in 1960; increased life expectancy meant that most parents had years together in an "empty nest" after their children had left home; at midcentury women began childbearing at a later age and bore fewer children than in 1900. In addition, economic changes in the decades following World War II led women, including married women and women with children, into the paid labor force in unprecedented numbers. This drew women out of the home for part of the day and gave them greater economic independence. The introduction of the birth-control pill in the 1960s gave women more control over pregnancy, and the ability to plan the timing of their children's births encouraged women to work outside the home and to think of careers rather than just temporary jobs.

These and related changes provoked a dramatic transformation of divorce law between 1965 and 1974. Herbert Jacob has called the adoption of no-fault divorce the "silent revolution": revolution because it involved a series of "radical changes in legal expectations about family life"; silent because the changes resulted from "routine" policy processes that never became the focus of media and public attention.

In the mid-1960s lawyers in California began the push for no-fault divorce in large part to get rid of the subterfuge that took place in many divorce proceedings, in which couples would tailor their stories to fit the legal requirements for divorce. Although California courts were lenient in granting divorce, in order to obtain a divorce a husband or wife had to prove that the other had committed an offense such as adultery, cruelty, willful neglect, habitual intemperance, or desertion. In most cases the wife was the plaintiff, and she usually charged her husband with cruelty, which could range from disparaging remarks to physical violence. The charges were often fabricated and the testimony rehearsed, the couple having agreed to end the marriage. The dishonesty, even perjury, that pervaded some divorce proceedings prompted activists to press the legislature to adopt a no-fault divorce law, which enabled a spouse to obtain a divorce without proving wrongdoing by the other.

No-fault divorce emerged before modern feminism, and its proponents did not aim to promote greater equality for women or greater choice among alternative family forms. Nor did they plan or anticipate the demographic watershed in U.S. families that resulted from no-fault divorce. In the wake of no-fault legislation the divorce rate rose dramatically, from 2.2 per thousand people in 1960 to 4.8 per thousand people in 1975. And by the last quarter of the twentieth century only one-fourth of U.S. households fit the supposed norm of a wage-earning husband and homemaking wife living with children.

Alongside its dramatic demographic consequences, no-fault divorce prompted a sea change in conventional understandings of marriage. The idea that marriage partners themselves could simply decide to end their marriage was revolutionary; it affected thinking about the very nature of marriage and its permanence. The observation by the nineteenth-century legal historian Henry Maine that the movement of the law in the nineteenth century was "a movement from Status to Contract" was finally coming to be true of marriage.

Although no-fault divorce preceded the resurgence of feminism, the idea that individuals should be able to extricate themselves from unhappy marriages resonated with feminist ideas about women's liberty and equality—and later with the movement by gays and lesbians to end legal discrimination against homosexuals and the ban on same-sex marriage. The conjunction of no-fault divorce, renewed attention to equality, and gay liberation, as Nancy Cott observed, sparked proposals to "reinvent marriage" by "extend[ing] its founding principle of consent between the couple to all the terms of the relationship, allowing the contractual side of the hybrid institution to bloom." If personal choice suffices to end a marriage, why, the contractualist asks, shouldn't personal choice define the terms of marriage from the outset?

II. A Third Wave of Reform?

Marriage and Liberty

Liberty, the first foundational value of a liberal polity, is central to the question of who is allowed to marry. When the law stipulates who may and who may not marry, it restricts the freedom of those excluded from marriage. Some exclusions are relatively uncontroversial, such as prohibiting marriage below a certain age, with a close relative, or while in prison (although each of these has been attacked as an unjustifiable limitation on individual freedom). Other restrictions are more contentious. The law precluded slaves from marrying. And only in 1967, in the case of *Loving v. Virginia*, did the Supreme Court decide that antimiscegenation laws were unconstitutional.

Advocates of contract marriage favor legal recognition of same-sex marriage, a position consistent with their dedication to individual liberty. Because marriage has a public status, they say, the law inevitably draws a line separating those who may marry and those who may not. The repeated refusal by states to formalize unions of same-sex couples represents, according to the contractualists, a failure to take pluralism, privacy, and personal choice seriously. States, of course, may enforce agreements between marriage partners just as states enforce other contracts; and they may prohibit marriages below a certain age just as they impose age restrictions on other contracts. But states may not legitimately decide who may marry whom or how spouses should order the personal and material aspects of their relationship.

I might be tempted to become a contractualist if contract marriage were the only way to achieve legal recognition for same-sex marriage, but—as current political initiatives at the state level underscore—it is not. Marriage for same-sex couples can be achieved either by legislation or by court decisions that change the content of marriage law; we need not replace a regime of marriage law with a regime of private contracts. The fact that many municipalities have adopted "domestic partnerships" and that Vermont has recognized "civil unions" may be a harbinger of legislative victories to come. And courts may someday decide that there is a constitutionally protected right to marry that encompasses same-sex couples. The ground was laid in *Loving v. Virginia* when the Supreme Court declared, "The freedom to marry has long been recognized as one of the vital personal rights essential to the orderly pursuit of happiness by free men. Marriage is one of the 'basic civil rights of man,' fundamental to our very existence and survival." If marriage is a fundamental liberty protected by the Fourteenth Amendment's due-process clause, then any restriction on marriage must be tailored to advance a compelling state interest. And while some religious views may condemn homosexual unions, no state interest rises to a sufficiently compelling level to justify prohibiting same-sex marriage.

The debate here is not between those who are for and those who are against same-sex marriage but between contractualists, who would provide legal recognition of same-sex marriage by abolishing marriage law, and people who would instead alter marriage law itself. Is there any reason to prefer the latter? I think there is.

The individualism and emphasis on rational bargaining that are at the heart of contracts rest on misleading models of the person and of the marriage relationship. Marriage partners are not only autonomous decision makers; they are fundamentally social beings who will inevitably experience need, change, and dependency in the course of their lives. The prenuptial agreements that set forth how the economic assets each partner brings to a marriage are to be held and distributed recognize the individuality of the partners, although they strike some people as unromantic. But the question of who should have a claim to property obtained by either spouse during the course of a marriage is more problematic because when people marry they become part of an entity that is not entirely reducible to its individual components. Some states determine all such property to be held in common (community property), reflecting the notion that marriage creates a single entity and a shared fate (and hence shared resources). Other states give title to the person who earned or otherwise obtained the property but allow title to be overridden in the interests of a fair distribution at the time of divorce, reflecting a belief that marriage creates claims growing out of a shared life. The relational entity is also reflected in common language when spouses say they are doing something "for the sake of the marriage," such as choosing a place to live that would be neither partner's first choice if single. It is reflected in legal practice when one spouse is prohibited from testifying against the other in certain proceedings because the law wants to express the notion that the marriage relationship itself should be protected.

Married life is not only deeply relational but also unpredictable. Not all of what spouses may properly expect of one another can be stipulated in advance. Contracts are useful devices for facilitating communication about each partner's expectations and aspirations. But contracts create obligations by volition and agreement; they do not account well for the obligations that may arise from unforeseen circumstances, such as the illness or disability of an aging parent, a spouse, or a child.

Finally, contractualism suggests that each marriage is a particular agreement between individuals, not a relationship in which the public has a legitimate interest. But the public does have an interest in the terms of marriage. It has, as the equal status view argues, an interest in promoting equality of husband and wife, both as spouses and as citizens, and in securing what Martha Nussbaum calls the social bases of liberty and self-respect for all family members.[3] And it has an interest in sustaining marital and other family relationships in the face of poverty or illness.

One way to think about the differences in these two approaches is to consider whether polygamy should be legalized in the United States. As the *Boston Globe* columnist Jeff Jacoby asks, "If the state has no right to deny a marriage license to would-be spouses of the same sex, on what reason-

able grounds could it deny a marriage to would-be spouses
. . . who happen to number three or four instead of two?"
Would a continuation of the ban on plural marriage simply
shift the boundary between who's in and who's out?

For contractualists, the case for a right to plural marriage is straightforward: it expresses individuals' rights to
form affective and sexual relationships free from state interference. Martha Fineman wrote in 2001 that "if no form of
sexual affiliation is state preferred, subsidized, and protected,
none could or should be prohibited. Same-sex partners and
others forming a variety of other sexual arrangements would
simply be viewed as equivalent forms of privately preferred
sexual connection." The law would have to be gender-neutral, allowing marriages with plural husbands as well as plural wives. But as long as protections against coercion, fraud,
and other abuses that invalidate any contract were enforced,
people could choose multiple marriage partners.

Proponents of the equal status conception fall on both
sides of the question. Laurence Tribe, supporting the legal
recognition of polygamy, asks rhetorically in *American Constitutional Law* whether the goal of preserving monogamous marriage is "sufficiently compelling, and the refusal
to exempt Mormons sufficiently crucial to the goal's attain-
ment, to warrant the resulting burden on religious con-
science." Peggy Cooper Davis condemns in *Neglected Stories*
the "cultural myopia" that led the Supreme Court to outlaw
Mormon polygamy in *Reynolds v. United States* in 1879 and
argues that a principled objection to polygamy in a multicul-
tural society would require more than "a political majority's

wish to define and freeze the moral character of the polity." But the flaws in the *Reynolds* decision do not mean polygamy should be legalized. Many people are convinced that polygamy is profoundly patriarchal. What Davis calls the "larger cultural context of female subordination" may be too strong and deeply rooted for even gender-neutral principles allowing both women and men to have more than one spouse to overcome its effects. In this view, plural marriage reinforces female subordination and is unacceptable on the grounds of equality.

The answer to the question, If we legalize same-sex marriage, won't we have to legalize plural marriage? is not, then, an obvious "yes." Equality as well as liberty is implicated in marriage law and policy. In assuming the equal agency of the parties to the contract, the contract model leaves aside the question of whether choices themselves may lead to subordination. In order to decide whether plural marriage should be legalized, one must address the question of whether polygamy can be reformed along egalitarian lines. Equality must be a central attribute of any marital regime based on considerations of justice.

Marriage and Equality

Most people today endorse "equality" as a general cultural value, but there is deep disagreement about what kind of spousal equality we want and how best to achieve it. Advocates of gay and lesbian marriage who are concerned principally with restrictive rules about who may marry whom typically do not engage this issue. But a vision of the proper relationship between spouses is central to the conservative project; a compelling alternative to it will require its own core vision.

Under nineteenth-century marriage law the fact that a wife's legal personality was subsumed in that of her husband, that she was not able to vote, and that she was excluded from many occupations was regarded by many not as inequality but as complementary difference. Today some traditionalists contend that although men and women, husbands and wives should enjoy equal rights both in marriage and as citizens, they have different roles to play in family and civil society. For example, Chad Brand explains the Southern Baptist Convention's position that "while the Bible teaches full equality, it does *not* affirm egalitarianism or interchangeability in all things." He contends that "male-female equality and male headship may seem paradoxical, but they are both taught in Scripture, much like a thread of two strands."[4] In a secular vein William Kristol asserts that women and men must be taught "to grasp the following three points: the necessity of marriage, the importance of good morals, and the necessity of inequality within marriage."[5] Because the nation needs strong and even aggressive men to flourish, the price women pay for marriage and morals is submission to the husband as leader within the family.

Angered by the endorsement of male dominance in these views, advocates of contract marriage such as Martha Fineman argue that "abolishing marriage as a legal category is a step necessary for gender equality." Marriage by contract replaces the gender stereotyping and protectionism of traditional marriage law with the recognition of the individuality and equal agency of the partners. Marriage partners should be treated as rational actors capable of knowing and articulating their interests. Contract reflects autonomy and self-direction in general, and marriage partners are individuals who, according to the American Law Institute's Principles of the Law of Family Dissolution, need to "accommodate their particular needs and circumstances by contractually altering or confirming the legal rights and obligations that would otherwise arise."[6]

Supporters of contract marriage are right to reject male dominance and state protectionism. But as Carole Pateman argued in *The Sexual Contract*, while contract may be the enemy of status it alone is not adequate to defeat the legacy of patriarchy. The contract model is an insufficient foundation for spousal equality. Ensuring conditions of fair contracts is not in itself enough to establish this kind of equality in marriage and in civic life. Instead, marriage law and public policy must work to ensure that neither partner is precluded from participating in social and political life or rendered unable to provide care to family members. Vigorous state action is needed to promote spousal equality, and one important justification for such action is provided by a vision of marriage as a relationship between equals that enriches both their individual and joint lives. While marriage and divorce laws themselves are now usually drafted in gender-neutral terms, cultural norms and employment practices perpetuate a division of labor at work and at home that results in a system of gender and racial hierarchy. So even if reforms are animated by concerns about joining domestic equality with special respect for marital bonds, those reforms will need to focus on the labor market as much as the domestic arena.

Most jobs, whether professional or nonprofessional, still assume the model of what Joan Williams in *Unbending Gender* calls the "ideal worker," a full-time, paid employee married to an at-home caregiver. Employment practices in the United States developed around the sexual division of labor. Jobs were designated "male" or "female," and men's jobs tended to pay higher wages than women's. Even men and women doing the same work were paid according to different scales (men being presumed to be the family providers, women to be working for "pin money"). Health, unemployment, and other benefits were tied to full-time work. The workday and workweek were based on the assumption that someone else was cleaning, cooking, and caring for family members. The ideal worker model had enormous influence on both the economic resources and caregiving skills of men and women.

Although discrimination against women in the workplace has diminished, the ideal worker model continues to affect both decisions to marry and the dynamics within marriages. As Susan Okin argues in *Justice, Gender, and the Family*, the difference in wage-earning capacity between men and women gives men more resources with which to deal with the world, and this in turn affects dynamics within the family. The disparity still remains despite a narrowing wage differential between men and women of all races: while women in 1979 earned 62.5 cents for every dollar men earned, in 1998 they earned 76 cents. Because uninterrupted time in the work force increases one's potential earning power, wives who stay out of the paid labor force for a number of years fall behind. This diminishes their decision-making authority within marriage and their ability to leave an unsatisfactory union.

The arrangement of the workplace also affects decisions about caregiving, for children as well as elderly or sick relatives. Because benefits such as health insurance may depend on full-time work, and because the pay scale is often higher for full-time work, one partner may have to work full time. Because many jobs are sex segregated, and wages for men's jobs are higher than those for women's, it will make economic sense in some families for the husband to work full time and his wife to do the caregiving. The division between workers and caregivers not only harms women in the workplace but makes it less likely that men will develop interpersonal and caregiving skills.

In the Supreme Court's recent decision upholding one man's right to sue the State of Nevada under the Family and Medical Leave Act after his request for family leave to take care of his sick wife was denied, Justice Rehnquist noted the effects on both home and workplace of the assumption that women's role as caregivers frees men to be ideal workers:

> Because employers continued to regard the family as the woman's domain, they often denied men similar accommodations or discouraged them from taking leave. These mutually reinforcing stereotypes created a self-fulfilling cycle of discrimination that forced women to continue to assume the role of primary family caregiver, and fostered employers' stereotypical views about women's commitment to work and their value as employees.

[*Nevada Department of Human Resources v. Hibbs*, 538
U.S. 721, decided May 27, 2003]

Congress acted reasonably, Justice Rehnquist ruled, in mandating a family leave that would help to break these stereo-
types about male and female social roles. The tight linkage
between work and family is influenced not only by gender
but also by race and class.

Racial prejudice meant that, historically, fewer black than
white families had an "ideal worker" and a stay-at-home
caregiver. The economic need created by racial discrimination meant that the labor force participation of married black
women was always higher than that of white women. Black
men were relegated disproportionately to agricultural and
other low-paid labor, black women to domestic and other
service jobs. Since the last decade of the twentieth century
the high unemployment rate among black males has had
an additional impact on family life, as marriage rates have
fallen: William Julius Wilson, Orlando Patterson, and others
have argued that some people won't marry when they have
no reasonable hope of being able to support a family.[7]

As to social class, the increasing number of never-mar-
ried mothers living in poverty led the authors of the Welfare
Reform Act of 1996 (the Personal Responsibility and Work
Opportunity Act) to insert a provision requiring mothers
who receive welfare to identify the biological fathers of their
children. The state could then go after the father for child support, and if he did not provide enough money to lift mother
and child out of poverty, the mother would be required

to work outside the home. The sponsors hoped that if the woman identified the father the state might induce them to marry. Even if they did not marry, the man and not the government would then support the child. Many women eligible for welfare, however, did not want to identify the fathers of their children, some because they preferred to parent with someone else or alone, some because they feared abuse from the father, and some because they knew the father had no money (and often no job).

Marriage is not an effective antipoverty program, nor is it appropriate to use it as such. Unemployment rates are high because the number of jobs that pay a living wage is far below the number of unemployed people seeking work. The wages available to many men who can find work are inadequate to support a family, and adding a wife's wages is of little help unless affordable child care is available. Addressing women's poverty by attaching them to men who can support them reinforces inequality and vulnerability within marriages. Inducing women to marry men may expose them and their children to domestic violence while failing to provide them with either the personal or community resources to extricate themselves from intolerable living conditions.

The understanding of marriage as a contract does not by itself generate the reforms necessary to alter family and workplace structures, welfare, and social services in ways necessary to give both men and women the opportunity to engage in both public and caregiving work. The next phase of the struggle to achieve sexual and spousal equality must entail a public commitment to liberty and equality and tackle not only marriage law but economic circumstances as well.

A number of reforms would move society toward greater justice in marriage. One such reform would be to ensure that people can find jobs that pay a living wage. There must be equal pay for equal work, whether performed by full- or part-time employees. Benefits must be extended to all workers, not just those who meet the ideal worker model (and basic health benefits should not be tied to employment status). Work must also be restructured in such a way that it accommodates caregiving, through a shorter workweek and more flexible scheduling, for example. If caregivers are not to be marginalized, high-quality, affordable child care must be part of any comprehensive family policy, as must the kind of child allowance common in European countries. Paid parental leave for both men and women would create an incentive for men to participate in child care, particularly if a father could not transfer his leave time to someone else but had to use it or forego the benefit. In the event of divorce the wages of both a primary wage earner and a primary caregiver should be treated as joint property, reflecting the commonality of marriage, particularly if there are children or other dependents.

These measures certainly do not exhaust the possibilities. They illustrate the point that in order to meet the principle of spousal equality men and women alike must be able to perform the tasks necessary to both the public and the private realm, to shoulder the responsibilities of workers outside the home as well as family caregivers.

III. Public Status or Individual Contract?

The contractual image has much to be said for it. It captures what Milton Regan Jr. in *Alone Together* calls the "external stance" toward marriage, which focuses on the ways in which marriage serves the interests of distinct individuals. The contract model represents well the role that choice and negotiation play in any marriage. Drafting a marriage contract is a useful exercise for a couple because it encourages potential partners to assess their individual needs and sources of personal satisfaction, make their expectations explicit, and identify areas of both agreement and conflict. Legal notions of spousal unity and the sentimentalization of a woman's role as "the angel in the house" have often served to undercut married women's agency and autonomy. The external stance provides an important antidote.

Contractualism does less well in capturing what Regan calls the "internal stance" toward marriage, which regards it from within the relationship and focuses on shared experience rather than lives lived in parallel association. The internal stance reflects the fact that when people marry they become part of an entity that is not reducible to or identical with its individual components. Historically this concept of a marital entity distinct from either spouse was oppressive to women. The doctrine that husband and wife were "one" and formed a new "person" in the eyes of the law deprived married women of their independent right to hold property and enter into contracts in their own name until the latter half of the nineteenth century. Prior to the advent of no-fault divorce in the late 1960s a court had to find that one of the spouses had committed an offense "against the marriage" before granting a divorce. Incompatibility was not a valid ground for divorce even when both partners wanted to end their marriage. Even in our own day police may ignore complaints of domestic violence because they do not want to "intrude" on the private realm of the married couple.

Despite this dismal history, the notion that marriage creates an entity that is not reducible to the individual spouses captures a truth about significant human relationships and could be used to reshape social and economic institutions in desirable ways. This understanding of the marriage relationship could be used in the future not to subordinate women but to press for marriage partners' rights to social and economic supports that sustain family relationships and enable spouses to provide care to one another. Such a right to provide care to and receive care from a spouse is not the same as an individual's right to health care or social services. Nor does public protection and support for associational and affective ties need to be limited to marriage partners and parents and children. Rather, recognition of the inevitability of dependency and the importance of caregiving should lead people to ask what other relationships deserve public support.

Marriage as a status suggests, as the contract model does not, the role of committed relationships in shaping the self. The promise to love someone else, in a marriage or in a friendship or in a community, binds a person to act in ways that will fulfill that obligation. A contract also does not express the notion of unconditional commitment, either to the other person or to the relationship. Contract in lieu of marriage rests upon a notion of quid pro quo, in which each party offers something and agrees on the terms of an exchange as a rational bargainer. But the marriage commitment is unpredictable and open ended, and the obligations it gives rise to cannot be fully stated in advance. What love attuned to the well-being of another may require is by its nature unpredictable.

With so much of our public discourse reducing individuals primarily to consumers in the market, it is especially important to insist on the social and relational sides of our lives. The contractual model, which presents marriage, as Hendrik Hartog writes in *Man and Wife in America*, as "nothing more than a private choice and as a collection of private practices," is insufficient to the tasks of reconfiguring marriage. Marriage entails respect for individuals and for their relationships. It is a particularly striking instance of a practice founded on both individuality and "a shared purpose that transcends the self" (Regan). If such a commitment is a valuable aspiration and one that our political community wants to facilitate, then we need to examine and remove impediments to such relationships. Those impediments are legion, especially among the poor. Removing them thus confronts us with a formidable agenda—reforming the workplace, welfare, and caregiving. But with the notions of public good and collective responsibility under constant assault, withdrawing the state from the pursuit of justice in marriage and family moves us in the wrong direction. We need to insist instead that marriage and family law can and must be made to conform to the principles of justice that affirm the equality and equal liberty of all citizens.

Notes

1. In Jewish law, marriage involved a contract (*ketubah*) in which a man accepted a woman as his wife in exchange for a bride price and pledged a specific amount of money to her if he divorced her. Divorce was only available to the man. The blessings of the wedding ceremony invoked a more covenantal relationship, but the contract was essential to marriage. The Jewish contractual law of marriage was different both from Christian law, which by and large did not permit divorce, and from views of secular contractualists that I examine here.

2. *Chapman v. Mitchell*, 223 N.J. Misc. 358 at 359–60, 44 A. 2d 392 at 393, quoted in Herbert Jacob, *Silent Revolution: The Transformation of Divorce Law in the United States* (University of Chicago Press, 1988), 6.

3. Martha C. Nussbaum, "The Future of Feminist Liberalism," in Eva Feder Kittay and Ellen K. Feder, eds., *The Subject of Care* (Rowman and Littlefield, 2002), 192.

4. Chad Brand, "Christ-Centered Marriages: Husbands and Wives Complementing One Another," September 1998, www.baptist2baptist .net/sbclifearticles/sept%5F98/sept%5F98.html (accessed 6 June 2003).

5. Quoted in June Carbone, "Is the Gender Divide Unbridgeable? The Implications for Social Equality," *Iowa Journal of Gender, Race, and Justice* 5:31 (fall 2001): 73.

6. Quoted in Martha Albertson Fineman, "Marriage and Meanings," in Anita Bernstein, ed., *Why Marriage?* (New York University Press, 2005). Fineman has written extensively on contract marriage, including *The Neutered Mother, the Sexual Family and Other Twentieth Century Tragedies* (Routledge, 1995).

7. Wilson is right to assert that ending unemployment is imperative, but decent-paying jobs for men alone will not foster spousal equality in either black or white families. Unless jobs are available for women as well, and unless both men and women are provided with

the means to combine wage labor and family caregiving, spousal relations will continue to be hierarchical and unequal. Orlando Patterson writes in *The Ordeal of Integration* about conflicts between black men and women that have caused the marriage rate among black Americans to decline.

Originally published in the summer 2003 issue of *Boston Review*.

Nancy F. Cott

The Public Stake

Marriage is paradoxical and perhaps unique in legal terms because it involves both a contract and a status, although these two concepts are distinct—almost opposite—legally. It has been this way ever since monogamous marriage was codified in Europe between the sixteenth and eighteenth centuries, first by ecclesiastical and then by secular authorities. A contract is characteristically consensual, joined by private agreement. No contract need be exactly like another, since the parties themselves decide on its substance and extent. A status, on the other hand, means a legal standing fixed by public authority, attaching certain rights or limitations to those in a defined group or class. (A minor's status differs from an adult's, for example, and a citizen's from a noncitizen's.)

Marriage has both features. Two individuals who consent to marry form a contract that continues when they marry and thus enter a new status. In other words, the contract of marriage is no ordinary contract. The state is a party to it along with the couple, authorizing the marriage and mandating its form and some of its terms, preventing the couple from making the contract fully their own. The involvement of state authority also implies that the public supports the couple's bond, will enforce it, and values it as something worthwhile to the community at large.

It is this third-party role of governmental authority that contractualists would excise from marriage and that Shanley wants to keep in. From the contractualist point of view, the public status of marriage is the dead hand of the past, constraining the ways individuals form relationships and households. Not necessarily, Shanley replies. She embraces a principle that conservatives have taken for granted: the public has a stake in marriage; eliminating it would be more loss than gain. Unlike conservatives, though, she would make the purposes of public authority in marriage newly supple and generous, directed toward egalitarian goals.

Under the glare of her spotlight, the contractualist solution shrivels. Yet is her alternative efficacious? Shanley's aim to renovate the public and social dimensions of marriage rather than concede these to conservatives gives her essay its energy. But I find Shanley's approach too mired in her opponents'—that is, the contractualists'—emphasis on individual lives and agency. In order to meet the contractualists on their own ground, Shanley looks mainly inside putative marriages, where, she argues, considerable liberty and a greater likelihood of equality can flow from enlightened government involvement. But with one exception (the exclusion of polygamous unions) the laudable purposes she has in mind (such as promoting the equality of men and women in their relationships, sustaining households in the face of poverty, addressing sex segregation and wage gaps in the economy, and improving child care) do not depend on the state regulating marriage. In fact, marriage law seems an indirect way, and not the most desirable one, to pursue these goals. A state with these aims in the forefront could direct public policy toward workplaces and households and affect all men and women, married or not.

More fatally—if Shanley hopes to bring both conservatives and contractualists around to her view—she says too little about what the *public* gains from maintaining marriage as a public institution. A century ago, it seemed obvious to legislators, jurists, and social scientists why marriage meant government interposition. The notion that a government attentive to public good would *not* regulate marriage was "too absurd to require a word of refutation," according to Joel Bishop's *Commentaries on the Law of Marriage and Divorce*, the nineteenth century's most prominent American legal treatise on domestic relations. G. E. Howard's three-volume *History of Matrimonial Institutions* (1904) likewise assumed that "in no part of the whole range of human activity is there such imperative need of state interference and control as in the sphere of the matrimonial relations." Governments were instituted to create social order, and what could be more disorderly than unconstrained sex (in noncontracepting populations) and haphazard inheritance of private property? By stipulating and regulating monogamous marriage, governments corralled both these areas.

Today, the public benefit of government involvement in marriage no longer goes without saying. Shanley's premise, that marriage is "a relationship that transcends the individual lives of the partners," is not a self-evident justification for government to be involved. Shanley hardly queries the fact that the state's imprimatur on marriage makes it a very *privileged* status. Married couples get a huge stack of rights and benefits (along with a set of constraints), at a time when only slightly more than half the adult population is married.

For Shanley to persuade me, she would need to confront more directly the question of whether there is a public good in assigning these privileges to married couples only. There's the rub: a just marriage policy can arise only from a clear definition of the public good, built on a vital sense of the collective public. It is not Shanley's problem alone that, in American law and policy today, the collective public (unlike specialized interest groups) has only a fleeting presence. The ghost of the public interest has to be called back in more palpable form for a just marriage policy to be devised.

Joan C. Tronto

Marriage
Love or Care?

Mary Shanley makes a convincing case for choosing a middle way between the exclusionary conceptions of marriage offered by traditionalists and the overly permissive (and potentially inegalitarian) conceptions offered by pure contractualists. Yet while Shanley may have steered clear of Scylla and Charybdis here, these comments are written with an eye on the shoals up ahead. After all, the aspect of marriage that interests the liberal state (or any state) is not the intimate relationship between two consenting individuals but the more complex relationships among the generations that result from marriages, whether in producing children or caring for the elderly. Love and care are not the same, yet both affect our individual and collective interests, in both the short and the long term, in marriage.

Shanley's essay takes for granted that liberal societies take an interest in promoting the liberty of individual citizens. Thus, individuals should all have the same opportunities to create valuable and validated intimate relationships with others. The constraint that Shanley recognizes is that society must guarantee some degree of equality in these intimate relationships. Without it, Shanley argues, there is no guarantee that the parties are forming unions that further their interests as free individuals. Thus, in Shanley's argument, too, the concern for equality collapses into a concern for liberty.

Shanley's emphasis on the importance of liberty underplays an important alternative understanding of marriage and the family. Even within the liberal state, marriage looks very different from a structural, state's-eye view than it does from an individual's perspective. Here, the role of marriage is not so much to allow individuals to express their individuality as it is a way for the state to guarantee the care and nurturance of its newly born and immature citizens and the protection of its vulnerable elderly and infirm citizens.

When we look at marriage from the standpoint of the state's interests, the question of marriage becomes more complicated. On the one hand, it becomes clear that the state has interests apart from the protection of personal liberty in ensuring that marriages occur. The state can rely upon individuals to bear children and provide them with care during the first years of life. The state has an interest in guaranteeing that people marry, procreate, and take care of one another. Even John Stuart Mill argued in *On Liberty* that a marriage license should only be issued to those who can offer proof of their ability to pay for and take care of a child. So on one level, the state's stake in marriage is very high.

On the other hand, though, a century-long trend that British sociologists call "defamilization" has already seen many of the traditional functions of the family displaced by the state or other public institutions. For example, today the state makes enormous investments in its citizens' education, health, and welfare. Old-age pensions maintain the independence of elderly persons. Hospitals and nursing homes have removed birth and death from the household. Increasingly, even eating and food preparation are done outside the household. As households shrink in function, they also shrink in size. The average U.S. household is now 2.62 people, and 26 percent of households consist of only one person.

It is easy, however, to exaggerate this point, and not only because the neoliberal policies of many modern welfare states have attempted to control health costs by transferring as much care as possible back to the household. The family not only provides material support for its members (and especially its most vulnerable members) but is also a source of an individual's sense of identity: theories developed by Freud in the late nineteenth and early twentieth centuries envision the nuclear family as the source of all psychological resources and problems.

While the Freudian model describes the importance of the family in negative terms—that no one survives his or her growing up without psychological scars—the sense that the family contributes something fundamental to people's self-conceptions and that it provides a necessary safety net for vulnerable children seems inescapably true. Marriage is thus not only about love but also about care. The broader scope within which the discussion of marriage occurs, then, is the debate over care and whether it should be left to the family, an institution founded on love.

Utopian and dystopian thinkers have been the most creative in separating raising children from the intimate relationships of mature adults. Plato's *Republic* advocated a nonparental education for its guardians. B. F. Skinner, the anti-Freudian psychologist, posited in *Walden Two* a system of collective child-rearing that would replace the family, which he described as the "frailest of modern institutions." Feminists have often created nonfamilial utopias. Charlotte Perkins Gilman made all of the female citizens into collective mothers in *Herland*. Ursula K. LeGuin's *The Dispossessed* created separate quarters for children, though not all children found the arrangement of separating adult intimacy from parenting satisfying. Marge Piercy, in *Woman on the Edge of Time*, imagined an arrangement in which twelve-year-olds would go through a special ritual to choose their three mothers.

What would happen, then, if intimate human relationships no longer incorporated the raising of children or the protection of elderly or infirm relatives? Can we imagine family structures that would not only assign these sorts of care to outside institutions but also permit and encourage the creation of new forms of care? As we rethink marriage, we have a chance also to rethink radically what the family might be. From such a perspective gay marriage and a public standard for equality between spouses seem easy, if vital, first steps.

Cass R. Sunstein

Of Federalism and Caste

Mary Lyndon Shanley rejects the contractualist model of marriage. She believes that contractualism neglects the mutual dependence of spouses and the need for "positive state action to enhance equality and equal opportunity." In particular, she contends that marriage should be understood in such a way as not to subordinate women but "to press for marriage partners' rights to social and economic supports that sustain family relationships and enable spouses to provide care to one another."

I want to explore two gaps in Shanley's excellent paper.

1. Shanley is aware that states greatly vary in their approaches to the marital relationship, but she says little about how the variations might bear on law and policy. In

the 2000 campaign, Vice President Dick Cheney, asked about same-sex marriage, responded, "Different states are likely to come to different conclusions, and that's appropriate. I don't think there should necessarily be a federal policy in this area." I believe that the vice president's response was wise, and that the wisdom of his response extends far beyond the issue of same-sex marriage. Of course there should be decent floors, based on an understanding of people's minimal entitlements, moral and economic; states should not be permitted to forbid people to use contraceptives or to marry people of different races. (More on that shortly.) But beyond those floors, a great deal of variation should be welcomed.

There are two reasons to approve of variations across state lines. First, we need to learn a lot more about the nature and effects of possible arrangements, and the best way to do that is through experiments. For example, many people are fearful of same-sex marriage, believing that it will have harmful effects. If some states allow such marriages, the risks will be easier to evaluate. With respect to the possibilities for marriage, many experiments will be highly informative. Second, the United States has a great deal of heterogeneity on questions of value; our moral commitments are plural and conflicting. With respect to marriage, as elsewhere, some states will prove willing to be more adventurous than others. Different values in (say) Massachusetts and Utah argue in favor of diverse private and public arrangements.

Consider the extraordinary decision of the Supreme Judicial Court of Massachusetts, ruling that a prohibition on same-sex marriage violates the Massachusetts constitution. The Supreme Judicial Court was interpreting Massachusetts law, with that state's highly distinctive culture, constitution, and legal precedents. As the court emphasized, citizens of Massachusetts have often been held to have rights that go beyond those in the U.S. Constitution. (This is not rare; many state constitutions go beyond the national charter.) Importantly, the court hardly foreclosed political debate within the state. The Massachusetts Constitution can be amended relatively easily, far more so than the nation's. To approve of the court's decision, it is not necessary to be certain that as a matter of principle, same-sex unions should be permitted everywhere or even anywhere. It is necessary only to say that ours is a federal system and that reasonable people have made reasonable claims on behalf of those unions. The genius of the federal system lies in the fact that it allows law to adapt to the diverse cultures of diverse states—and simultaneously provides extensive room for experimentation and learning. The point holds for experiments that go well beyond the domain of same-sex relations. For example, heterosexuals, no less than homosexuals, might be permitted to enter into civil unions as well as marriage; many heterosexuals might in fact prefer that option, and some states should provide it to them.

2. What are the conceptions of liberty and equality for which Shanley means to speak? Those who favor the contractualist approach believe that they are promoting both liberty and equality. Shanley disagrees, emphasizing the need for reforms that go beyond contracts to embody a "public commitment to liberty and equality." But how are these ideals to be understood?

I suggest that Shanley has two ideas in mind. The first is a general right to freedom from desperate conditions. Arguing for a right to minimal economic security, Franklin Delano Roosevelt contended that necessitous people cannot be free. In 1944, he proposed a Second Bill of Rights that would have gone a long way toward the reforms that Shanley seeks. Roosevelt's catalogue included the right to a useful and remunerative job; the right to a decent home; the right to adequate medical care; the right to adequate protection in the event of old age, sickness, accident, and unemployment; the right to a good education. Notice that freedom from desperate conditions imposes duties on the state, not only (and perhaps not at all) on one or another spouse. Hence Shanley seeks to enable people "to extricate themselves from intolerable living conditions"—a point that of course extends far beyond the law governing marriage and the family.

But I think that Shanley is also interested in another ideal, one that we might describe as an anticaste principle. She wants to ensure that one group of people is not systematically subordinated to another. On this view, social practices and law should not turn a morally irrelevant characteristic into a systematic source of social disadvantage. The problem with race and sex inequality often consists of the creation of lower caste status—of practices, both public and private, that have the effect of putting one group systematically below another. With respect to women, that is exactly what the traditional law of marriage has done. If we want to retain marriage, and to go beyond contract, we will take steps to ensure that women do not turn out, in one or another respect, to be a kind of lower caste. The current law of marriage does not do nearly enough on this count; the same is true for institutions that govern children, welfare, and employment.

These points help to illuminate both the uses and the limitations of federalism in the context of marriage. Bans on same-sex marriage have been challenged on the ground that they create second-class citizenship and hence run afoul of the anticaste principle. The challenge is most straightforward when made by gays and lesbians, who are deprived of access to a central institution, but it has also been made by women as such, who contend that the ban is part of a system of sexual stereotyping that operates to subordinate women to men. Notably, ideas of this kind have started to play a role in judicial opinions—but in the opinions of state rather than federal courts.

Hence, the development and elaboration of the anticaste principle owes everything to the federal system. At the same time, that principle imposes some constraints on what states can do; no state should be allowed to subordinate women. Thus, an understanding of the requirements of the anticaste principle will call for protective "floors," in the name of both liberty and equality, below which no state can go. Elaboration of those floors will take a great deal of time and effort. But in the case of civil unions and same-sex marriage, at least, the situation is clear: experimentation at the state level is highly desirable, and it should not be stopped by national intervention.

Martha Albertson Fineman

Why Marriage?

Mary Lyndon Shanley seeks to fill a perceived gap between American conservatives, who decry the state of marriage in the United States, and their critics, for whom she seems to have much sympathy. She identifies as the primary problem a so-called lack of "alternatives" to the marriage-promotion movement and proposes a comprehensive plan that combines a love for equality with a respect for the institution of marriage. Unfortunately, Shanley's plan is as shortsighted as our government's family policies, evolved over a half century of "reform." An analysis that perpetuates the primacy of marriage excludes nonmarital relationships. At the same time, wishfully extolling the virtues of equality in marriage does nothing to implement it or to address the difficulties that many American families face.[1]

Law and policy in the United States already incorporate equality as the normative standard governing the relationship between married partners. Paradoxically, as equality within the family reigns on a symbolic level, the economic stability of real-life families has declined. Parents, married or not, now have to work longer and harder to provide necessities for their children. And still a significant portion of the population's children live in poverty or suffer deprivation of essential goods and protections, such as insurance. Those children, as well as many of the ill and elderly, are too often left with inadequate resources. Shanley's ideal of egalitarian marriage won't help these families, given their material need.

On a rhetorical level, the marital family is presented by politicians and pundits of the marriage movement as the very foundation of society—the institution upon which the national well-being, culture, and society rest. Such laudatory language is hypocritical, though, considering how the family is treated in law and policy.

Marriage is the way the United States privatizes dependency, giving the family the primary responsibility for providing for the needs of its members. Unlike other industrial democracies, in which the state assures some floor of social services to each citizen, in America individual needs are managed by the family unit. In a society in which employers are downsizing jobs and benefits, the burden is significant. The burden is not lessened by myopically focusing on family form and valorizing the union between husband and wife. The relationship between family and society—the responsibility of the state to provide basic social services—should be the focus of our concern.

When Shanley dismisses my call for the abolition of marriage as a legal category as a proposal for "contractual" relationships between adult partners, she misunderstands both my critique and the constructive dimensions of my argument. I am not concerned with the nature of the relationship between sexually affiliated adults—the husband-wife dyad. I have argued that such a focus distorts policy discussions, masking important issues concerning dependency and caretaking for those who are in need, including children and many of the elderly, the ill, and the disabled.[2]

In *The Illusion of Equality: The Rhetoric and Reality of Divorce Reform*, I argued for a version of the equal status that Shanley advocates, encouraging a paradigm shift away from formal equality toward a more substantive "equality of result."[3] I realized only later that such a shift was not possible when the subject of analysis was only the family and the relationships within it. The family cannot be transformed if the society in which it is contained remains profoundly unequal. To have equality within the family, there must be corresponding transformations in the institutions that shape the context and possibilities for the family. The ideology and policies governing both market and state must acknowledge that those institutions bear some responsibility for dependency in order for equality within and without the family to be possible.

It is not surprising, given the persistent masking of the caretaker–dependent crisis by marriage rhetoric, that advocacy for equality in the family is understood as part of the war between the sexes. As I noted in *The Neutered Mother, the Sexual Family, and Other Twentieth Century Tragedies*:

> As we face high divorce rates and the organization of women and men into gendered interest groups when confronting issues of intimacy, we should not be surprised that legal rules are considered prizes by competing factions. Law provides an arena for public, symbolic as well as real competition between groups of women and groups of men.[4]

But my point has been that this gendered organization is destructive of real reform.

In my most recent book, *The Autonomy Myth: A Theory of Dependency*, I argue that the metanarrative of romantic sexual affiliation has deflected or absorbed concern for nonhorizontal intimate connections, particularly the one between parent and child. The shared assumption is that the right kind of family is built around the heterosexual couple—a reproductive pairing that is regarded as divinely ordained in religion, crucial in social policy, and a normative imperative in ideology. It does not take much imagination to see whom this excludes; and this exclusion has profoundly detrimental effects on children and the elderly. The very phrase "single mother" implies that the "normal" mother is identified primarily in relation to her husband. In the rhetoric of those espousing children's rights, children's problems are created by being "trapped" in a "deviant" family situation, "prisoners" or "victims" of a family that is often "broken" through divorce, or "pathological" because it was never sanctioned by marriage.

Midway through Mary Lyndon Shanley's brief "history" of marital reform, she invokes an oft-cited statistic that should have made her stop and rethink her basic project. Citing the most recent census, she notes that "only one-fourth of U.S. households fit the 'norm' of a wage-earning husband and a homemaker wife living with children." So, one might ask, as a sheer matter of practicality, what should "family policy" have to say about all those others?

The state should be involved in supporting and subsidizing some family relationships. But the target of state policies should be the caretaker–dependent tie, not that between sexual affiliates. If our concern is with children, the question should not be how we can resuscitate marriage and thus save society and the traditional family, but how we can support all individuals who perform the important societal work of taking care of those who because of their age or physical or mental conditions are dependent upon some form of family.

Notes

1. In her concern for marriage, Shanley continues to adhere to the assumption that the primary family organization is an entity, built on and arising from the sexual affiliation of two adults. This heterosexual unit continues to be considered presumptively appropriate as the core family connection. At worst, heterosexual marriage is viewed as merely in need of some structural revisions. She is caught in a trap of focusing on gender equality to the exclusion of broader societal concerns.

2. See *The Neutered Mother, the Sexual Family, and Other Twentieth Century Tragedies* (1995), *The Illusion of Equality: The Rhetoric and Reality of Divorce Reform* (1991), and *The Autonomy Myth: A Theory of Dependency* (2004).

3. I argued in *The Illusion of Equality* that such reform would have to represent a shift from a relationship of equal status to a relationship of "equal outcome," or of results. There I wrote, "Marriage is no longer realistically presented as a lifelong commitment with well-defined gender-based roles establishing interdependency that is easily comprehended and reflected in supportive legal rules. Things are more complex today—roles are less defined, and marriage as an institution is in a state of flux. Unfortunately, the laws governing property distribution and other economic aspects of divorce have become the crude instruments by which we attempt *both to implement equality and to address dependency and need.* When the law is expected to do incompatible and contradictory things simultaneously, it is no wonder that confusion results" (p. 39).

4. *The Neutered Mother,* 148–49.

David B. Cruz

Mystification, Neutrality, and Same-Sex Couples in Marriage

In "Just Marriage," Mary Lyndon Shanley raises vital issues about the future of marriage and marriage law in the United States. In contrast to marriage exclusionists—my term, not hers—who would perpetuate the denial of civil marriage to same-sex couples, Professor Shanley would open civil marriage to adult couples regardless of the partners' sexes. Shanley's essay, however, is not primarily a response to marriage exclusionists. Rather, she aims to defend civil marriage against what she calls "contractualism"—primarily but not exclusively feminist calls for the abolition of marriage as a legal category and its replacement with a regime of private contracts for ordering the relationships of adult couples. Justice in marital relationships can better be achieved, Shanley argues, by transformations in law and policy than by abandoning marriage as a legal category.

I am sympathetic to Professor Shanley's project. Supporters of class, race, and sex equality must be impressed with Shanley's careful attention to the ways in which formally sex-neutral marriage laws are insufficient to assure equality in people's lived relationships. Moreover, as the experiences of many lesbian, gay, and bisexual persons have shown, it is simply not possible today for couples to assume all the legal consequences of civil marriage through private contracts, to which marriage exclusionists including George W. Bush seem intent upon relegating us.[1] When two persons marry, there are often legal effects upon third parties, who as a general matter cannot be bound by a private contract between two persons. In order for that to be possible, special state laws must be in place.

Still, I am uncertain about some aspects of Shanley's argument for mending rather than ending marriage. First, it is not clear to me why the case is well served by appealing to a mystical notion of marriage as an "entity" apart from the persons who marry. Second, I doubt that Shanley has answered all of the strong nonfeminist reasons some contractualists give for supporting the abolition of civil marriage. Third, I am not as sanguine as Professor Shanley about the prospects of same-sex couples achieving access to civil marriage throughout the nation.

I found one of the most curious features of Shanley's argument to be the insistence that contractualism's emphasis on individual liberty improperly fails to recognize that "when people marry they become part of an entity that is not always reducible to its individual components." Professor Shanley is generally a realist: she observes that "the sentimentalization of a woman's role as 'the angel in the house' [has] often served to undercut married women's agency and autonomy." And, following the law professor Joan Williams, she details a number of reforms that must be made to the structure of paid labor, health benefits, and marital-dissolution law if marriage is to become a just institution in practice.

But the essay is replete with what strikes me as a dangerous conception of marriage as an entity, a conception that I worry romanticizes the debate and obfuscates the stakes. Almost every point Shanley wishes to make about marital commitment can, I believe, be made with reference to the marrying partners and without invocation of a marital "entity." Certainly one does not need to ontologize a marital relationship, which after all is a *relationship* between individuals, to conclude that "spouses can make claims . . . that are not identical to the claims that each could make as individuals." One does not need to hold "that marriage creates a single entity" to believe that persons who marry each other create "a shared fate (and hence shared resources)." We can recognize that a marriage may be a commitment, a relationship, a valuable way for two individuals to order their lives, without having to mystify this relationship. And, as Shanley notes, similar metaphoric treatment of marriage as creating a "unity" between spouses has historically underlain unjust marriage laws.

Shanley may be correct that a similar notion of marriage-as-entity could be used in the future "to press for marriage partners' rights to social and economic supports that sustain family relationships and enable spouses to provide care to one another." Yet one need not postulate a freestanding entity to press for such changes, and people might well deploy the notion for unjust ends. (Modern natural-law theorists defend the exclusion of same-sex couples from civil marriage in large part on the religious or mystical notion that marriage creates a "two in one flesh" union.) At the very least, I think more work must be done before Shanley may assert that it is a "*fact* that when people marry they become part of an entity" (emphasis added).

This criticism somewhat deflates Professor Shanley's arguments against contractualism, some of which appear to rely on contractualism's inhospitability toward the notion of a marriage entity. But rhetoric matters, and Shanley may in the end be right that the individualist language and tradition of contract law foster a mindset that does not optimally reinforce "the social and relational side of our lives." But I do not think Shanley takes on one of the most powerful liberal arguments for abolishing the legal category of marriage. Some contractualists believe that civil marriage improperly privileges one particular form of intimacy—the adult, sexually involved dyad—at the expense of other forms, thus presumptively violating the proper liberal neutrality about the good life. While Shanley thoughtfully explores functional reasons states might have for rejecting polygamy, the essay at best obliquely approaches the issue of the neutrality of the liberal state. If one thought that polygamy restrictions tend improperly to align the state with one conception of the good life, further argument might be necessary to show that defending the right (that is, combating sex-based subordination) might justify this limitation on people's choices concerning the good.

Finally, Shanley notes that she would be more sympathetic to contractualism "if contract marriage were the only way to achieve legal recognition for same-sex marriage." Yet, at the time "Just Marriage" was written, "current political initiatives at the state level" suggested to her that "marriage for same-sex couples can be achieved by either legislation or court decisions that change the content of marriage law." Since that time, courts in Arizona and New Jersey have rejected constitutional claims for access to marriage; the decision of the Supreme Judicial Court of Massachusetts insisting on marriage rights for same-sex couples has prompted a state constitutional convention where opponents of the ruling hope to defeat it; the proposed Federal Marriage Amendment, which among other things would forever declare marriage to be between partners of opposite sexes, went from having 25 to almost 100 sponsors in the House of Representatives; and President Bush has repeatedly invoked the possible need for "the people" to turn to "the constitutional process" to keep courts from "redefining" marriage.

All this suggests that it might not be so easy for same-sex couples to prevail in our claims for access to civil marriage. But that may not be a telling criticism of Shanley's arguments. A heterosexually identified supermajority whose (occluded) view of justice would deny same-sex couples the right to marry is not likely to give up its "special rights" by abolishing marriage and relying on contract laws neutrally available to all. In the end, then, Shanley may be right to urge the campaign for just marriage.

Note

1. See, e.g., Jennifer 8. Lee, "Congressman Says Bush Open to States' Bolstering Gay Rights," *New York Times*, February 9, 2004.

William N. Eskridge Jr.

The Relational Case for Same-Sex Marriage

The case for same-sex marriage has been most power-
fully supported by reference to liberal premises: adults
presumptively ought to be able to choose their own marital partner, and the state ought to recognize such unions of
choice on an equal basis. Because many mature adults would
like to form lasting commitments to sexual partners of the
same sex, the state ought to recognize same-sex marriages.[1]
The case against same-sex marriage has been most power-
fully supported by reference to communitarian premises:
the state should guide individuals to make good choices and
should limit choices that have bad effects on third parties or
on society. Because same-sex marriage is not a worthy aspiration in the way different-sex (man–woman) marriage is,

the state should discourage and may prohibit the former.[2] Most Americans still oppose same-sex marriage for reasons such as these.

One of the things I have learned from the same-sex marriage debate is that the liberal conception of self—the foundation for the contract model criticized in Professor Shanley's article—is not, standing alone, a persuasive basis for thinking about human happiness and well-being.[3] We are not just autonomous bundles of exogenously defined preferences seeking satisfaction. We are also social beings struggling to make connections, including lasting connections, with one another. Our selves and our preferences are shaped in significant ways by the care our parents gave us and by the interactions we enjoy with our adult partners and our own children, relatives, and coworkers. This is what one might call the *relational self*, a complement as much as a competitor to the *rational self* of the contract model. The most persuasive defense of state-sponsored marriage against the individual contracts is that it remains, for many people, an institution that valorizes ongoing relationships that have deep significance for society as well as individuals.

One powerful argument against same-sex marriage is that it will be a state stamp of approval of the "homosexual lifestyle," which critics maintain is a bad aspiration for adults and a baleful influence on children. The deepest aspiration for coupled adults is man–woman marriage, and any other signal is both misleading and pernicious. Supporters of same-sex marriage have traditionally belittled this argument as an unrealistic understanding of the power of the state to inculcate specified life choices in the young. But assume that state marriage laws do send normative signals that have a genuine impact on the mores of our nation's youth. Is there still a case for same-sex marriage?

Yes. Lesbian and gay couples ought to receive state stamps of approval, since they can benefit from the unitive features of marriage just as much as straight couples can.[4] Everyone knows gay couples who have found meaning as well as family in their commitment to a shared life. Preliminary social-science evidence supports that intuition. Dr. Lawrence Kurdek's 1998 study of the ongoing relationships of 239 heterosexual couples, 79 gay male couples, and 51 lesbian couples is the most ambitious statistical analysis of couples to date. Controlling for the other major variables, Kurdek found that the quality of the relationships over time was comparable for the gay male and straight couples, and that the lesbian couples showed a significantly higher quality of relationship after five years.[5] The last finding suggests that same-sex marriage may have an additional social benefit by providing new insights into what is a productive family. If woman–woman partnerships can produce unusually bonded arrangements that yield high satisfaction to women, different-sex partnerships (and even man–man partnerships) might learn something. In short, same-sex couples are not only acceptable role models, they might be better role models than many out there now.

Dr. Kurdek also found that the gay male and lesbian couples had a significantly higher separation rate than the straight couples, all of whom were married. While it is notable that most of the lesbian and gay male partnerships endured, Kurdek speculated that the lower endurance rate was due to the lack of social and legal supports for same-sex unions. It is reasonable to believe that legal recognition of same-sex marriages, especially if accompanied by gradual social acceptance, would enhance the durability of lesbian and gay relationships. From a communitarian perspective, this would be a boon, for the relational self yearns for connections that have legs. In short, the state's stigmatization of gay unions undermines gay interpersonal commitment, albeit to an indeterminable extent.

If that is so, state denigration of lesbian and gay relationships often harms children. Thousands of children are being raised in lesbian and gay households today. Studies have suggested—again, provisionally—that lesbian parents are doing a very good job raising these children.[6] Assume it is true, as traditionalists do, that children benefit from having two parents rather than just one. Assume, further, that state denigration of lesbian and gay partnerships undermines their longevity. In that event, the state is contributing to the break-up of some lesbian and gay families rearing children—to the detriment of the children. To put the matter more positively, by denying gay men and lesbians the right to marry, the state is foregoing an opportunity to reinforce the stability of the two-parent household for the children of those relationships.

Notes

1. See, e.g., William N. Eskridge Jr., *The Case for Same-Sex Marriage* (1996); Morris Kaplan, *Sexual Justice: Democratic Citizenship and the Politics of Desire* (1997); Richard Mohr, *A More Perfect Union:*

Why Straight America Must Stand Up for Gay Rights, ch. 3 (1994); Mary Coombs, "Sexual Dis-Orientation: Transgendered People and Same-Sex Marriage," 8 *UCLA Women's Law Journal* 219 (1998).

2. See, e.g., Richard A. Posner, *Sex and Reason* 311–13 (1992); C. Sydney Buchanan, "Same-Sex Marriage: The Linchpin Issue," 10 *University of Dayton Law Review* 541, 567 (1985); John Finnis, "Law, Morality, and 'Sexual Orientation,'" 69 *Notre Dame Law Review* 1051–53 (1994). See also *Marriage and Same-Sex Unions: A Debate* (Lynn Wardle et al., eds., 2003).

3. I more fully developed the ideas that follow in William N. Eskridge Jr., *Gaylaw: Challenging the Apartheid of the Closet* 278–88 (1999). I acknowledge a big debt to Milton C. Regan Jr., the author of *Family Law and the Pursuit of Intimacy* (1993).

4. See Laura Benkov, *Reinventing the Family: The Emerging Story of Lesbian and Gay Parents* (1994); Michael Sandel, "Moral Argument and Liberal Toleration: Abortion and Homosexuality," 77 *California Law Review* 521 (1989); Carlos Ball, "Moral Foundations for a Discourse on Same-Sex Marriage: Looking Beyond Political Liberalism," 85 *Georgetown Law Journal* 1872 (1997).

5. Lawrence Kurdek, "Relationship Outcomes and Their Predictors: Longitudinal Evidence from Heterosexual Married, Gay Cohabiting, and Lesbian Cohabiting Couples," 60 *Journal of Marriage and the Family* 553 (1998).

6. See Judith Stacey and Timothy Biblarz, "(How) Does the Sexual Orientation of Parents Matter?" 66 *American Sociology Review* 159 (2001) (meta-analysis of the empirical literature studying children raised in lesbian households).

Amitai Etzioni

A Communitarian Position
for Civil Unions

Professor Shanley's argument is compelling, powerful, and well grounded in communitarian arguments. However, when all is said and done she does not directly address the question of whether gay and lesbian unions should be accorded the same legal status as heterosexual ones. I could go on and on about why I so strongly agree with her analysis, as far as it goes. Marriages indeed are not private events; they are occasions in which a couple comes before a community to make a commitment that falls in line with the values of that community. They are also the coming together of two families, not just two individuals.

Above all the commitment is not contractual but open ended. There is a world of difference between an agreement

63

to exchange services—you will take out the garbage and I will cook, you will take care of the children on even days and I on odd days, you will care for me when I am sick and I for you when you are sick—and a commitment to be together through thick and thin. No one in her right ("rational") mind would stick to a contract when the other partner has advanced cancer, AIDS, or dementia. There is no return to be expected, and the burden is overwhelming. If marriage were a contract and these circumstances arose, one would look for ways to wiggle out of the contract or accept the penalty and move on. However, most marriage partners stay put in such circumstances because the marriage "contract" (a very misleading term) contains a moral obligation that is much more binding than contracts. It is indeed a covenant.

To replace marital covenants with private contracts is to burn down the house to accommodate some new tenants. But they would have no house either, once marriage becomes akin to an economic deal. A marriage based on agreed arrangements would be as vacuous for homosexuals as it would be for all others.

So far, I am just underscoring what Professor Shanley has said so well. She is, however, surprisingly vague about whether these public commitments should be framed differently for heterosexuals and homosexuals. Before I can directly answer that question I need to make a general point about a communitarian approach to politics. (I keep referring to "a" communitarian position because I of course speak only for this communitarian. Communitarians differ on this issue even more than other bodies of thought.) The point is that society, unlike philosophy, cannot be derived or based on one overarching principle. A libertarian philosophy can be built around the primacy of liberty (or autonomous choices) and also the assumption that all that does not suit it can be treated as wrong, or at least as a deviation, at best as a bad compromise needed for expedient considerations.

In contrast, society appears to have values that cannot be fully realized nor made fully compatible because of the diversity of its members and their interests and needs. In principle, society must find ways to accommodate differences without going whole hog in one direction or the other. We cannot maximize liberty or equality. We must find ways for gun owners who believe that owning guns is part of their birthright to live with those who, like me, feel strongly that guns are evil incarnate. Communitarian politics hence entails finding ways for people of different basic values to live together without one set of values "trumping" the other. Much democratic politics reflects such communitarian treatment of basic differences.

In the case at hand, many gay people feel strongly that unless they are entitled to exactly the same marriages as heterosexuals, their basic individual rights are violated, which they (and many liberals) hold as semisacred. Many social conservatives feel that gay marriages drive a stake through their hearts and violate all that is holy to them. Civil unions—if made available to both gays and heterosexuals who want to signal a different form of commitment than traditional marriages—are a reasonable middle ground. (Indeed, societies are moving to form still other types of "marriages," such as those that are limited by time or those with or without children. Louisiana introduced a still different form—the covenant of marriage.)

Civil unions accord those involved in them *most* of what traditional marriages provide: the right to inherit, share health benefits, and so on. Indeed, ceremonies and public commitments can be made for civil unions too. And such unions allow social conservatives to believe that that which is sacred to them has been respected. Such a compromise is not the best of all worlds, but it is the best that one can achieve in our society at this stage in history. We must respect other members of our community the way that we wish for them to respect us.

Milton C. Regan Jr.

Between Justice and Commitment

In "Just Marriage," Mary Shanley offers a perspective on marriage that builds on both liberal and communitarian insights. On the one hand, she argues that genuine equality between spouses should be an essential feature of marriage. Her analysis illuminates how commitment to this goal requires measures that go beyond the regulation of marriage per se to encompass reforms in the workplace and in social-benefit programs. On the other hand, Shanley accepts the view that society has an interest in treating marriage as a public institution. That institution embodies the ways in which intimate relationships can shape the identities of those within them and can generate dependencies and responsibilities that are not purely the product of individual choice.

Shanley, in other words, is not willing for liberals to concede all the communitarian ground to social conservatives who support marriage as organized along traditional gender lines. We can, she argues, take steps to promote genuine equality within marriage while simultaneously insisting that marriage is not a matter of purely private concern. That is, gender equality is possible by reforming marriage as a social institution rather than replacing it with a regime of contracts.

One way to describe Shanley's approach is to say that she believes that society can promote both justice and commitment in marriage. She is especially eloquent on the importance of justice and how law might promote it. She elaborates somewhat less, however, on why commitment is important and how law might promote it. I'd like to expand on both those points a bit.

First, why should commitment in marriage be a substantive value that we encourage? One obvious answer, of course, is to protect children and financially dependent spouses. Divorce can have profound economic and emotional effects on these persons that are of concern to all of us. From this perspective, commitment is valuable in an instrumental sense—as a way of promoting the welfare of those who are vulnerable to injury from divorce.

But is intimate commitment a good thing in itself? Suppose, for instance, that we could devote enough resources to protect children and financially dependent spouses from significant injury at divorce. Or, to isolate commitment as an intrinsic value even more starkly, suppose that two adults of comparable economic means wish to end their marriage. Does society have an interest in either case in encouraging partners to think seriously about whether to end their relationship? Or is it just their own business?

There is a good argument to be made that a society does have an interest in promoting commitment per se. Indeed, that value can be especially important in liberal societies that place a high value on the individual. For a person to have a sense of herself as a distinct individual over time, she must be able to make and keep commitments. A commitment represents the deliberate narrowing of future courses of action for the sake of a purpose that a person regards as integral to her sense of identity. By freely accepting certain constraints on her possible courses of action, an individual expresses who she is.

In this sense, a person does not merely have commitments; rather she is defined by them. Her core commitments are, to use Lynn McFall's terms, "identity-conferring."[1] They reflect what we take to be most important and become "premises of our agency."[2] Rather than simply being a self that is indiscriminately pulled by every stimulus and experience, a person is able to construct a personal narrative in which her actions have purpose and meaning. Her commitments provide some evaluative distance from the demands of the immediate present and thus sustain a sense of individual continuity.

Several features of modern social life make it more difficult to create and sustain such continuity. Advances in communications technology and the accelerating pace of daily life create a sense of "time-space compression"[3] that intensifies individuals' exposure to multiple stimuli. Mass consumer society depends crucially on eroding the ethos of deferred gratification that was the foundation of the older capitalist order. Furthermore, many sectors of the economy have adopted flexible production methods designed to respond rapidly to shifts in market conditions. These have dislodged the predictable linear career path and have substituted in its place a discontinuous roller-coaster ride that requires individuals to constantly "retool" and "reinvent" themselves.

All these forces contribute to a heightened sense of impermanence and discontinuity in everyday experience, creating a world in which the present seems only dimly connected to either the past or the future. Such fragmentation makes it difficult to sustain commitment and thus stable identity. Because of this, it's appropriate for liberal societies to treat commitment as a substantive value worth promoting. It's not that commitment is instrumental in maintaining coherent identity. Rather, as I've suggested, it's integral to the very concept itself.

Even if we grant this claim, though, does the legal institution of marriage promote this good? At first glance, there is some reason to be skeptical. Marriage law over the past generation has become increasingly laissez-faire. Law now generally prescribes no particular behavior on the part of spouses. Prohibitions on adultery, for instance, have largely been eliminated, and those that remain are virtually never enforced. The state's ability to establish requirements for entering into marriage has diminished in the wake of the Supreme Court's pronouncement that marriage is a fundamental constitutional right. In almost every state, a spouse can unilaterally seek divorce without the need to justify his or her decision beyond the claim that the marriage is effectively beyond repair.

Furthermore, spouses have the authority to enter into a contract that would divide financial resources between them in the event of divorce, thus superceding state rules that would otherwise govern the matter. Courts generally enforce such contracts, usually requiring only that they have been entered into voluntarily. In this respect, state divorce laws on financial allocations between spouses have become default rules, applicable only if the spouses have not expressed their own preferences on the matter. Some might thus argue that we have already moved a considerable distance toward a contractual approach to marriage. Would taking the last step be such a large change?

To be sure, courts don't grant divorcing spouses comparable discretion with respect to children. Agreements relating to child support or custody receive more stringent review to ensure that they adequately provide for the child's best interest. But a contractual regime would likely not change this significantly. Conventional contract doctrines, such as solicitude for third parties affected by the contract and sensitivity to public policy, would be available to protect children. Furthermore, intimate partners in a contractual regime who did not enter into agreements regarding the end of their relationship nonetheless would likely be subject to obligations on the ground that they were parties to an "implied" contract. In this respect, the parties would not be penalized by the absence of marriage.

Thus, even if we accept the substantive value of commitment in intimate relationships, one might argue that direct state involvement in marriage doesn't promote that value much more than would a regime of contracts.

The significance of marriage, however, isn't necessarily exhausted by its specific legal consequences. As a social institution, marriage plays a crucial role in serving as an impersonal source of value that can give meaning to personal choice. As Charles Taylor has suggested, individuals make choices against the backdrop of a "horizon" of significance that delineates what society deems important.[4] The sense that something has value depends upon the conviction that its worth and importance are impersonal. As Stephen Darwall puts it, "That which endows our life with meaning must be something whose value we regard as self-transcendent."[5]

Marriage serves this process of social validation with respect to the value of commitment. It bestows on partners a formal legal status that is the basis for impersonal rights and obligations. As David Chambers puts it, "Marriage is the single most significant communal ceremony of belonging."[6] Those who marry participate in a public ritual that marks entry into an institution that dwarfs any particular couple's experience. Lawrence Blum's concept of "role morality"[7] suggests the way in which marriage combines elements of personal and impersonal value. Those who identify with the values and ideals of a role have a personal stake in carrying out its obligations. A well-defined social institution such as marriage can evoke personal identification with the impersonal value of intimate commitment. Marriage's historical resonance makes it a powerful vehicle for expressing this value. By entering a social institution that has endured over numerous generations, individuals orient themselves within a distinct cultural narrative in which self-realization is linked with intimate attachment.

As Shanley suggests, the norms of this social institution need not be static. While long-term commitment has been a relatively stable feature of marriage, the roles of men and women within it have changed. Many couples now aspire to an egalitarian marriage, although failure to take the kinds of steps that Shanley suggests makes it hard to realize that vision. Furthermore, claims for recognition of same-sex marriage have prompted a vibrant debate about the values that marriage should serve. Those claims have underscored that same-sex couples desire not simply the material benefits of marriage but the social affirmation and support that comes from an emotionally powerful social institution. Substituting a contractual regime for marriage could thus deprive us of something that both embodies and helps reinforce the value of intimate commitment.

In sum, Mary Shanley is right to argue that we need not dismantle marriage in order to promote equality in intimate relationships. If we address the broader social, economic, and legal forces that shape spouses' behavior and choices, we can take steps that will help reform this social institution. Marital justice, in other words, need not come at the expense of marital commitment.

Notes

1. Lynne McFall, "Integrity," 98 *Ethics* 5, 13 (1987–88).

2. Jeffrey Blustein, *Care and Commitment: Taking the Personal Point of View* 231 (1991).

3. David Harvey, *The Conditions of Postmodernity: An Enquiry into the Origins of Cultural Change* 240 (1989).

4. Charles Taylor, *The Ethics of Authenticity* 37 (1992).

5. Stephen L. Darwall, *Impartial Reason* 165 (1983).

6. David L. Chambers, "What If? The Legal Consequences of Marriage and the Legal Needs of Lesbian and Gay Male Couples," 95 *Michigan Law Review* 450 (1996).

7. Lawrence A. Blum, "Vocation, Friendship, and Community: Limitations of the Personal-Impersonal Framework," in *Identity, Character, and Morality: Essays in Moral Psychology* 173, 178 (Owen Flanagan and Amelie Oskenberg Rorty, eds., 1990).

Elizabeth F. Emens

Just Monogamy?

Right now, marriage and monogamy feature prominently on the public stage. Efforts to lift state and federal prohibitions on same-sex marriage have inspired people across the political spectrum to speak about the virtues of monogamy's core institution and to express views on who should be included within it.

In this brief comment, I want to talk about something else. Like an "unmannerly wedding guest,"[1] I want to invite the reader to pause amidst the whirlwind of marriage talk, to think about alternatives to monogamy. In particular, I want to talk about multiparty relationships, or "polyamory," as these relationships are called by some of their participants.

Before doing so, I should acknowledge that I do not think that same-sex marriage will lead ineluctably to multiparty marriage. Our cultural commitment to the pair, the couple, the idea of total mutual love between two individuals, runs deep. Moreover, to design multiparty marriage would be a complicated legal endeavor, and the state may arguably have an interest in maintaining the efficiency of a relationship in which each person names just one other as a partner for all legal purposes.[2]

But regardless of what happens with the legal category of marriage, individuals in multiparty relationships are affected by many laws favoring monogamy, including adultery and bigamy statutes, domestic partnership schemes, zoning laws, custody laws, and adoption laws, to name a few. And those in multiparty relationships face severe normative censure. For this reason, among others, we should squarely confront the question of what constitutes multiparty relationships and whether we should proscribe them to the extent that we now do.

Contrary to what Shanley describes as the view of "many people," multiparty relationships need not be "profoundly patriarchal." When thinking of such relationships, most people think of polygamy, and more particularly, polygyny: one man married to multiple wives. I want to make two points about polygyny. First, the criminal law is available to address polygyny's worst-case scenario—which I take to be the coercion of underage girls into marriage and sexual relations. If the girls truly have not consented, or are incapable of consent, then the power of the state should be brought to bear on their persecutors. And if the legal age of consent to marry is too low to make consent a meaningful concept here, then the age of consent should be raised.

Second, polygyny, like monogamous marriage, also has a best-case scenario. One version of it is described in an article by Elizabeth Joseph, a Utah lawyer, who lived in a polygynous marriage of nine wives until the recent death of her husband.[3] For Joseph, polygyny is a "whole solution" to the problems of the modern woman trying to balance career and family.[4] Joseph cherishes the fact that, when she goes off to her full-time job as an attorney, her daughter is cared for at home by one of the other wives whom the daughter adores. In this respect, the charge that polygyny is oppressive to women is contingent; the validity of the charge depends on the individual relationship, just as in monogamous marriage. The very social changes that Shanley boldly proposes in order to make monogamous marriage an egalitarian institution—such as equal pay for equal work and high-quality affordable child care—are also the social conditions that would facilitate the most appealing version of polygyny.

Perhaps less familiar than these points about polygyny, for many readers, is the existence of an entirely different model of multiparty relationships called "polyamory." Polyamory is the practice of sustaining sexual, loving relationships among more than two. Called "ethical nonmonogamy" by some,[5] polyamory is viewed by its adherents as an alternative to the frequent practice of promised monogamy accompanied by sexual "cheating" behavior.[6]

Polyamorous relationships can involve just men, just women, or both men and women. The relationships' size and shape, and the types of bonds among the individuals, are as varied as the people who form them. For instance, three women may form a closed group of exclusive partners; two men and a woman may share a household in which only the different-sex pairs have sex; three men and a woman may form a family in which the woman sleeps with only one of the men, and the men all sleep with each other and are open to outside sexual partners. These are only a tiny sample of the various forms of polyamorous relationships.

Polyamorists aspire to what I understand to be five core values, some of which they share with many monogamists: (1) possessing oneself rather than trying to possess others; (2) self-knowledge, both about one's own desires for monogamy or nonmonogamy and as the basis for honest communication; (3) radical honesty, both about nonmonogamous practices and desires and about one's feelings and needs more generally; (4) consent between the partners to the rules and priorities of the relationship(s); and (5) privileging more sexual and loving experiences over other activities and emotions such as jealousy.[7]

This last point, perhaps the only one unique to polyamorists, deserves further explication. In brief, the cultural law of monogamy—as well as our actual laws[8]—privileges sexual exclusivity over an individual partner's desires for intimate sexual contact beyond the relationship. In romantic relationships, as opposed to friendships, jealousy trumps extrarelationship intimacy. That is, if someone is jealous of her friend's other friends, we tend to think the jealous friend should get over her jealousy. In a romantic relationship, the opposite is true: if a lover is jealous of his lover's other lovers, we tend to think the unfaithful lover should get over her extrarelationship desires and dalliances. The point may be taken further: if the lover were not jealous of his lover's other lovers, we might think that he should be.[9]

Polyamorists challenge this logic. They tend to think that jealousy can and should be overcome by open honest communication and self-interrogation about the source of the jealousy. They have a concept called *compersion*, which might be understood as the opposite of jealousy: pleasure taken in a partner's outside pleasures. They also point out various less obvious aspects of jealousy, like the fact that jealousy might not be necessary, particularly if we could imagine a world in which a "cuckold" was not imagined as betrayed but was instead understood as deriving pleasure from his partner's experiences, and as having extrarelationship satisfaction himself.

Most Americans probably do not want to have openly intimate relationships between more than two. Although most can presumably imagine desiring more than one person, their wish to avoid jealousy may exceed their wish to indulge their nonmonogamous desires. So they opt for monogamy, at least as a goal.

But the existence of some number of people choosing to live polyamorous lives should prompt us all to think harder about this issue. It should prompt us to think about our own choices and about the ways that our norms and laws urge upon us one model rather than pressing us to make informed, affirmative choices about what might best suit our needs and desires. At a moment when same-sex couples rush toward the altar, I suggest that we take this opportunity to question the desirability and the justice of monogamy's law.

Notes

1. Michael Warner, *The Trouble with Normal: Sex, Politics, and the Ethics of Queer Life* 119–20 (1999).

2. See Mary Anne Case, "What Stake Do Heterosexual Women Have in the Same-Sex Marriage / Domestic Partner / Civil Union Debates?" 37–38 (unpublished manuscript, on file with author).

3. See Dawn House, "Wives of Dead Polygamist Rebuild Their Lives," *Salt Lake Tribune*, Feb. 24, 2002, http://www.polygamyinfo .com/plygmedia%2002%2029trib.htm.

4. Elizabeth Joseph, "My Husband's Nine Wives," *New York Times*, May 23, 1991, at A31.

5. E.g., "Loving More, About Polyamory," at http://www.lovemore .com/aboutpoly.html.

6. For obvious reasons, reliable statistics on the prevalence of adultery are hard to obtain. The U.S. studies report that anywhere from 20 to 75 percent of adults have committed adultery. See, e.g., David L. Weis, "Interpersonal Heterosexual Behaviors (United States)," in *International Encyclopedia of Sexology* (Robert T. Francoeur, ed., 1997), http://www2.hu-berlin.de/sexology/ (citing E. Berscheid, "Emotion," in *Close Relationships* 110 (H. H. Kelley et al., eds., 1983); Judith Mackay, "Global Sex: Sexuality and Sexual Practices Around the World," Fifth Congress of the European Federation of Sexology, Berlin, 29 June–2 July 2000, at http://www2.hu-berlin.de/sexology/.

7. See Elizabeth F. Emens, "Monogamy's Law: Compulsory Monogamy and Polyamorous Existence," 29 *NYU Review of Law and Social Change* 36–44 (forthcoming 2004).

8. At least twenty-three states still have laws criminalizing adultery in some form, and forty-four states have statutes criminalizing bigamy.

9. For a fuller discussion of the complexity of responses to the idea of polyamory, see Emens, "Monogamy's Law."

Drucilla Cornell

The Public Supports of Love

I agree with Mary Shanley that family and kinship are and should remain irreducible to contractual relationships. Indeed I agree with her that contractualism, as a solution to the dilemmas of heterosexual marriage, turns on a psychoanalytically naive conception of the person, one that assumes that people are independent and bounded individuals from birth, and perhaps even more naively, that people are ever rational when it comes to sexual relationships. In the end, that is my disagreement with sexual "rationalists" such as Richard Posner in *Sex and Reason*.

Shanley, however, narrows the range of reforms of family law to a choice between contractualism and state-supported marriage that promotes the equal-status view of the lovers (including gay men and lesbians) in the marriage. (I am using the word *lovers* here, not *partners* or *stakeholders*, because Shanley is, at least implicitly, emphasizing the importance of ritual and other forms of commitment that bind people together.) But by defining the debate as between contractualists and conservatives who support complementary but unequal gender roles in a monogamous heterosexual marriage, Shanley misses some of the most pressing points made by critics of the legal establishment of heterosexual marriage as the publicly accepted and legally enforced norm of the family. Queer theorists have pointed out that marriage cannot be reformed because normalized heterosexuality packages us into contained gender roles that limit our freedom.[1] It is freedom from this containment, even within marriage, not equality between the genders, that queer theory advocates. Queer theorists deride heterosexual monogamous marriage as a hotbed of pomposity and hypocrisy, and as one of the great illusions of heterosexuality.

Shanley's reduction of the field of debate not only leads her to shrug off the searing critique of queer theorists; it also leads her to incorrectly designate feminist critics of heterosexual marriage, such as Martha Fineman, as contractualists. Fineman is far from that. Her entire argument is that the publicly supported form of the family should be the mother-child dyad broadly understood as a metaphor, and that this family should be given all the economic and social support necessary for raising children and for respecting caretakers. Fineman wants to break up the confluence of family and sexuality forced on us by the state through its regulation of the heterosexual family as the norm; she does not ultimately want to turn families into contractual partnerships à la Richard Posner.

Despite her brave critique of monogamous heterosexual marriage, Fineman's vision of the mother-child dyad is psychoanalytically naive. Indeed, as many feminist psychoanalysts have reminded us, the very idea of a relationship demands two differentiated human beings.[2] Trying to simply reenact the dyadic fantasy with mother and child (instead of husband and wife), even as metaphor, not only gets us nowhere new, it is also ultimately detrimental to the respect for mothers as persons that Fineman seeks to promote.

So what are we to do? I have argued elsewhere that we should defend as a moral and legal right the right of the imaginary domain, which would allow different forms of relationships to achieve the public status of marriage, including heterosexual marriage if the individuals happen to be heterosexual.[3] The right of the imaginary domain gives to the person the right of self-representation of their basic identifications as long as those identifications do not involve the denial of personhood to other citizens. For example, a "straight" person certainly has the right to identify as straight. But they don't have, under the imaginary domain, the right to define their "straightness" so as to forbid gays and lesbians the right to marry. I call the limit on the imaginary domain the degradation prohibition. I mean degradation in a specific sense. The degradation prohibition prohibits the denial of the status of personhood to other citizens in the name of any of their identifications of who they are. Think again of the example of gay and lesbian marriage. The right of gays and lesbians to marry, and the self-representations of gays and lesbians within that right, in no way takes away any of the fundamental rights of straight people. But the imaginary domain still forbids the state to legislate any particular definition of the "good" family, and thus the only legally protected family.

In the end, all of us need care and support. The real answer to that need is not simply to include plural marriage, understood as polygamy and polyandry, even if I argue that the state may not out of hand forbid either of these forms of marriage. More importantly we need to advocate different forms of plural marriage, specifically different forms of family relationships between adults, such as, for example, between three single mothers who are not lovers but who have thrown in their lot together as a family. Fineman is surely right that having sex with another adult does not necessarily make a family, although it can make children. Indeed, many children do not live in traditional monogamous, heterosexual families. As a society, we take care of many children without families through a contractual relationship between the state and its citizens called the foster-care system. Social worker after social worker has testified to the horror of that form of relationship and to the detrimental effects on many of the children who have survived it.[4] People in many societies, including notably African Americans within our own, have long lived in extended kinship systems that effectively function as families, even if they do not fit Shanley's reformed equal-status marriage.[5]

On a recent trip to South Africa, I visited a family run by Mama Amelia that embraced 101 children, of which she has legally adopted approximately 50; the adoption of the others is under way. It is not an institution run by the state. The relationship between Mama Amelia and her children is not contractual. The adults who live with her are all family members but are not all lovers, although she does have a boyfriend who is part of the family. Mama Amelia is part of a program in South Africa called Mothers for Others, one of the many organizations supported by the grassroots NGO Ikamva Labantu (Future of Our Nation). Mothers for Others is not an episode out of an Ursula K. LeGuin novel; it is a real, on-the-ground alternative to heterosexual, monogamous marriage as the only way to form a life of love and commitment.

People who seek monogamous heterosexual marriages should certainly be free to do so (on this point I disagree with Fineman), but of course that freedom has long been recognized, despite the reality, as Shanley notes, that women remain far from free or equal in heterosexual marriages as they are now conceived and realized. The real issue that has been put before us is the allowance of new forms of marriage and family such as the one provided by Mama Amelia and the adults with whom she shares the love of her children. In the end, it is not only important, as Shanley would have it, to recognize the significance of sentimental unions and ritualized bonds in human life (though I agree that such recognition is necessary), but also to move away from a family policy that makes the nuclear family (whether or not gay and lesbian marriage is to be included) the only state-legitimated form of family. Love, in the end, demands that we stretch our imagination to see new possibilities for kinship and learn from those that already exist.

Notes

1. See Judith Butler, *Gender Trouble* (New York: Routledge, 1989), and Michael Warner, *The Trouble with Normal* (Cambridge: Harvard University Press, 2000).

2. See Jessica Benjamin, *Bonds of Love* (New York: Pantheon, 1988).

3. Drucilla Cornell, *Imaginary Domain* (New York: Routledge, 1995) and *At the Heart of Freedom* (Princeton: Princeton University Press, 1998).

4. Judith Stacey, *In the Name of the Family* (Boston: Beacon, 1996).

5. See Carol Stack, *All Our Kin: Strategies for Survival in a Black Community* (New York: Harper and Row, 1974).

Wendy Brown

After Marriage

The track record for marriage as a just institution, Shanley is the first to admit, is a poor one. Historically, marriage has promulgated neither liberty nor equality but rather has been and remains a site of male and heterosexual superordination. So why attempt to produce justice at this site? Because, Shanley insists, marriage promotes enduring associational and affective ties, "represents the social and relational sides of our lives," makes people "part of an entity that is not reducible to or identical with its individual components," and, as such, constitutes a reprieve from a radically individualistic order of rationality and action.

To eliminate the gender subordination in marriage and homosexual exclusion from it, Shanley advocates a number of political and economic reforms. These include the introduction of gay marriage and "jobs that pay a living wage . . . equal pay for equal work . . . benefits extended to all workers . . . basic health benefits not tied to employment status . . . work restructured in such a way that it accommodates caregiving through a shorter workweek and more flexible scheduling . . . affordable child care . . . the kind of child allowance common in European countries . . . paid parental leave for both men and women." For Shanley, these reforms are desirable because they "move society toward greater justice in marriage." But why don't these add up to a formula for justice, period? Together these reforms would contribute to the historically unparalleled possibility of developing a modest, ungendered autonomy for adults that includes rather than eschews caring for children and other dependents. With them, intimate relationships of all sorts as well as the project of child-rearing would be less intertwined with the vicissitudes of economic life and would thus have better odds of thriving. Such reforms would end the subordinating economic dependency of women as caregivers in a capitalist political economy and relieve all individuals of fear for their well-being if struck by ill health or joblessness. By themselves, these goals are splendid, if unlikely. But why tie these reforms to marital justice? And why would or should marriage survive them as a kinship form? Why privilege marriage as *the* form for securing human relationality, enduring ties, and the value of being part of an entity larger than the individual? And why now?

It is common knowledge that the divorce rate is one-half the marriage rate in the United States today. Equally striking is the number of people in (sometimes secretly) unhappy, lonely, bitter, "dead," or otherwise unsatisfying marriages. These figures do not add up to a brief against marriage or marriage-like relationships, but they do remind us how terribly difficult such relationships are—indeed, how nearly impossible is the project of sustaining satisfying and enduring intimate relationships today given the psyches we bring to this project, the pressures to meet every need that is placed on it, the relative incompatibility between child-rearing and adult intimacy, and the lack of rich community sustenance for individuals and families alike. Nor does the difficulty of sustaining gratifying coupledom issue only or even primarily from gender inequality or homophobic exclusion, although these certainly compound it, as does the general ill fit between the organization of work in a capitalist society and the needs of families and individuals. But these are old problems and do not explain why marriage grows steadily more fragile and imperiled even as it remains idealized, sought after, and clung to. Late modernity brings us historically unparalleled deracination, evisceration of meaningful or stable work, attenuation of community, and, of course, erosion of the moral and religious forces promulgating the givenness of marriage. And as other sites of meaning and association have thinned, the point of life beyond survival has pretty much been reduced to individual gratification. It is in this context that marriages and families are expected to hold every flower in the bouquet of personal happiness and fulfillment—great sex, great children, great freedom, great adventure, along with love, excitement, fidelity, stability, and harmony—and not only are these impossible expectations, but marriages are often crushed by their weight, by the overburdened and claustrophobic character of the form.

Consequently, for many, the most important enduring associational and affective ties that sustain us are not marital, nor are they located in other traditional associations such as extended family or religious congregations. Rather, they are cobbled together from a modality of kinship to one side of both the contract and the marriage models Shanley discusses. This kinship is composed of the long-term friends to whom we have assigned guardianship of our children in case of our own death; with whom we celebrate holidays and birthdays; whom we ferry to knee surgeries and chemotherapy appointments and tend through days and weeks of emotional turmoil or physical illness. These are the friends whose phone calls we take in the middle of the night during break-ups with lovers, whom we prevent from disowning or drowning hair-raising adolescents, whose couches we sleep on and whose trucks we borrow, with whom we run marathons in middle age, whose children's college entrance essays we edit, whose accomplishments we celebrate, whose losses we mourn together. I am not describing "intentional communities" or utopian communes but rather webs of connection across households, often consisting of overlapping circles of friends rather than a single closed one and perhaps best described as a kind of loose extended tribe. While the texture and content of such tribes obviously varies across class and other stratifications, it may well include (as mine does) single parents, childless adults, married couples, homosexual parents, step-families, queer and straight loners, ex-lovers, selected neighbors, and grown children. Neither formal contract nor formal commitment establishes the endurance of these ties, but there is no doubt about their endurance. On the contrary, these ties are far more durable than most marriages and other couplings and yet enable those, too, when they are desired. Couples and families without this kind of kinship—those that attempt to make a complete relational world of their own on their own—are surely the most vulnerable to implosion, and to dire isolation afterward.

Do we need state recognition of such alternative kinship? Heaven forbid, although political consciousness and articulation of them could help us depart from the "marriage debates" in shaping agendas for gendered and sexual justice. Shanley's location of the public importance of private unions in marriage not only glosses the reality of marriage today, it occludes emerging ways of living and connecting to others that concretely embody commitment to "a shared purpose that transcends the self," ways that may have little relation to one's sexual life—be it serially monogamous, chaste, or promiscuous. If we are looking for the present and future possibilities of ties and associations that exceed the rationally choosing individual and also embody ambitions for justice, marriage would seem to be the least of these, and contract has nothing to do with them. Yet the more marriage is promoted as the privileged form in which our "relational sides" are recognized, the more invisible we will render other ways of committing ourselves to the well-being of others—ways, I would suggest, that would benefit from the political and economic reforms Shanley enumerates but are also already less normative, more egalitarian, and more "free" than the institution Shanley is working so desperately to save.

Shanley is right that enduring forms of "commonality" are crucial to human flourishing. She is also right that these forms cannot be produced by contract nor, really, from any part of a liberal or commercial table of values. But marriage does not represent, let alone exhaust, the current possibilities for meeting this need. And the continued political and economic privileging of marriage as *the* associational form probably relieves rather than produces pressure for the gender and sexual justice Shanley seeks. This privileging also relegates other modes of kinship to the status of shadowy background or poor substitute rather than sustaining and sustained forms of life beyond (but also inclusive of) the individual and the couple.

Brenda Cossman

Beyond Marriage

Mary Lyndon Shanley has made a compelling case
against the privatization of marriage and in favor
of the public interest in marital relationships. I agree that
the contract model is simply not up to the task of regulating these personal relationships and ensuring that relational
interests are protected. But to argue that relationships matter,
and that there is a broader public interest in protecting and
promoting relational interests, does not resolve the public-
policy question of how to regulate adult personal relationships, and whether marriage is the only or most appropriate way to recognize them. Shanley herself acknowledges the
importance of extending the analysis in arguing that "public
protection and support for associational and affective ties"

need not "be limited to marriage partners and parents and children. Rather, recognition of the inevitability of dependency and the importance of caregiving should lead people to ask what other relationships deserve public support." In these comments, I attempt to push this question forward and argue for a broader rethinking of the legal regulation of adult relationships.

Marriage has long been the system the law uses to recognize adult personal relationships. Relational rights and responsibilities—ranging from spousal support obligations and testimonial immunity to social security and employment benefits—have been extended on the basis of marital status. Public policy has assumed that marriage encompasses all the relational interests at stake in adult relationships—such as economic and emotional interdependency.

But marriage is both underinclusive and overinclusive in the promotion of these relational interests. While many marital relationships are characterized by a high degree of economic and emotional interdependency, some are not. Yet the full range of relational rights and responsibilities is nonetheless extended to these relationships. Conversely, many economically and emotionally interdependent relationships—such as same-sex couples and unmarried opposite-sex cohabiting couples—are excluded from these rights and responsibilities.

Many have argued for an expansion of the legal recognition of these otherwise excluded relationships. Some have suggested that the legal recognition of relationships should be expanded to include unmarried cohabiting couples. The American Law Institute's recent proposals for the legal recognition of de facto relationships, for example, follows the lead of other jurisdictions in which cohabitation has been increasingly assimilated into the regime of marriage. Similarly, many, including Shanley, have argued for the expansion of marriage itself to include same-sex couples.

These arguments for expansion are premised on the idea that these relationships should be recognized because they are marriage-like. Marriage thereby remains the norm and the standard for the legal recognition of adult personal relationships. This theory invites the question, What makes a relationship marriage-like? Shared residence? Sexual relationship? Emotional intimacy? Economic interdependency? Shared child-rearing?

Let's imagine two people who have lived together for twenty-five years. They own their house jointly. Their finances are intermingled. They are emotionally intimate. They share domestic responsibilities. They almost always socialize together. If they were married, the fact that they didn't have children wouldn't matter for the purposes of legal recognition. But let's say they aren't married. The American Law Institute proposal might include this couple for the purposes of some family laws. However, they would remain excluded from a range of public rights and responsibilities. Now let's say the couple isn't conjugal—the partners don't have a sexual relationship. Let's say they are two adult sisters. This couple would be excluded from the full panoply of public and private rights and responsibilities, notwithstanding the fact that their lives are characterized by precisely the same kind of emotional and economic interdependency as a married or cohabiting conjugal couple. The major difference is sex.

But should this couple be excluded from conflict-of-interest laws, or immigration laws, or support laws simply because they don't have a sexual relationship? Should the presence of a sexual relationship be the dividing line between those relationships that are recognized and those that are not? Is this in any way connected to the relational interests the law seeks to protect?

There is, I believe, a compelling case for rethinking the reliance on marriage and conjugality as the basis for the legal recognition of adult personal relationships.

The Law Commission of Canada has recently suggested a methodology for precisely this kind of rethinking.[1] It recommends a reevaluation of all laws and policies that govern the recognition of relationships with the following questions in mind:

1. Are the law's objectives valid? Maybe the law has extended beyond its period of relevancy and we'd be better off without it.

2. If the law's objectives are valid, do the relationships it governs matter? Sometimes relationships may be recognized in a context in which they really shouldn't matter.

3. If relationships do matter, can individuals be permitted to designate the relevant relationships themselves? Through a process of self-designation, individuals could choose who is most important to them, rather than have the state decide in advance who should be most important to them and therefore included.

4. If relationships matter and self-designation is not feasible or appropriate, is there a better way to include relation-

ships? Sometimes self-designation could be open to abuse. For example, it is not clear that individuals should determine for themselves who among their family or friends should be subject to conflict-of-interest rules. If so, then the question becomes whether there are better tests, tailored to specific statutory objectives that do not focus on marriage or conjugality. For example, instead of assuming that marriage is the appropriate test for inclusion, perhaps a test that focuses on emotional and economic interdependency would better capture the range of relationships that ought to be included.

This approach to rethinking the legal regulation of adult personal relationships is not one that requires abolishing marriage. Rather, marriage could continue to be one way in which individuals self-designate, or one way in which emotional and economic interdependency could be assumed. But it would no longer be the only way of designating inclusion. It would be an approach that would decenter marriage and conjugality from its privileged position as the only way of recognizing relationships and imposing relational rights and responsibilities. It would require a deeper examination of why relationships matter, a deeper examination that would demand thinking outside the marital and conjugal box.

As Shanley argues, withdrawing the state from family and relational life is not the path to justice. Relationships matter, and the state has a role in protecting and promoting those relational interests. Marriage is one way of doing so, but it shouldn't be the only way. The emotional and economic interdependencies of adult personal relationships create unique vulnerabilities. We ought to turn our attention to ensuring that these relational interests are protected wherever and with whomever they arise.

Note

1. Law Commission of Canada, *Beyond Conjugality: Recognizing and Supporting Close Personal Adult Relationships* (2001).

Tamara Metz

Why We Should Disestablish Marriage

Mary Shanley argues that to support stable caregiving unions, protect the vulnerable, and ensure gender equality, we must bolster but reform the legal institution of marriage. The alternative, she says, is to treat marriage as a private contract. But this approach, she warns, would fail to achieve the desired ends.

Shanley is correct about the limits of contract. The broader problem with contractualism is that it fails to capture the nature of—and therefore provide adequate protection and support for—*most* intimate caregiving relationships.[1] She is wrong, however, to conclude that protecting the vulnerable, supporting caregiving unions, and ensuring equality require bolstering the legal institution of marriage. On the contrary, these goals would be better served if the state withdrew from its current role of defining and conferring marital status. Liberty and equality, the vulnerable and their caregivers, married people and marriage itself would all be better served were marriage disestablished and a more general-purpose civil union aimed explicitly at protecting and supporting intimate caregiving units of all types created.[2]

To see why, we may begin with Shanley's familiar and compelling vision of marriage as more than a contract. But we cannot stop there. To decide what role the state should have in marriage, we must scrutinize the functions of public involvement more thoroughly than she does.

Shanley's position that marriage and equality are best served by reforming the legal institution of marriage rests on two assumptions: (1) that marital status carries a unique expressive value beyond the concrete and delineable benefits attached to it; (2) that this extra value depends on state definition and conferral of marital status. I agree with the first assumption but not the second.

What is this extra value, and does it rely on state involvement?

Shanley provides only the beginnings of an answer. Marriage is, she writes, "a special bond and public status." It is "a relationship that transcends the individual lives of the partners" in which the "public has a legitimate interest." But what exactly is the relationship between the public status of marriage and the transcendence it engenders? I propose that the extra value that Shanley attributes to marital status—and by an unnecessary segue, to state-defined and -controlled marital status—is what we might call *constitutive recognition*.

Marital status brings a complex, normative account both of the relationships it labels (between the two individuals and between the couple and the conferring community) and of the moral approval of the bestowing community. The public performance of this account has transformative and constitutive power by expressing the shared understandings of those involved. In short, the unique power of "marital" status is its transformative potential. This potential, in turn, depends on marital status being bestowed by an ethical authority.

We are more familiar with ethical authority in the realm of religion than in the realm of politics. The effectiveness of such authority, in the case of marriage, depends on a deep consensus concerning the meaning of marriage and, *crucially*, the belief that the conferring authority properly guides and decides the most intimate decisions (with whom one will partner, whether to dissolve such a union, and so forth) of those it governs.

If this is a fair description of the extra value Shanley attributes to marital status, we can see that her assumption that the state must control marital status if this value is to be realized is faulty. In fact, if this description is correct, then it seems that marriage would be better off if the state *did not* control the status. Why? Because, for both empirical and normative reasons, the liberal state is ill suited to serve as an ethical authority.

As a practical matter, while most Americans are familiar with the force of ethical authority, few if any experience the state as possessing authority of the kind just described. Thus, because of the tendency for the state to crowd out alternative sources of authority, the establishment of marriage robs marriage of the most effective sources of ethical authority (religious, cultural, secular, and informal civic groups). Were the state to withdraw from its current, contested role, alternative but more effective sources of ethical authority would likely fill the void.[3] To the extent that public recognition matters to its health, marriage and the goods it houses would thus benefit from its legal disestablishment.

Practical reasons in favor of disestablishing marriage stem from principled reasons. Ideally, the liberal state is relatively distant, more legal than moral, and more neutral than not among competing worldviews so as to protect individual freedom and diversity. Freeing marital status from the control of the state would thus be a boon for liberty. Just as the nonestablishment of religion protects diverse religious belief and expression, so too would the disestablishment of marriage protect competing views of marriage.

But what of the concrete public-welfare concerns—the protection of the vulnerable and the support of intimate caregiving units—that the state currently administers through marriage?

To say that the definition and conferral of marital status should be left to civil society is no different from saying that the control of *bat mitzvah* status should be left to civil society. In neither case do we assume that the state thereby withdraws from its role in protecting the vulnerable and promoting equality. What we *do* assume is that in a diverse, free society the state is primarily concerned with regulating action and not expression or thought.[4] The state must ensure that the vulnerable and their caregivers are protected.[5] On this point, we would be well advised to heed Martha Fineman's powerful argument in *The Neutered Mother* that the state's use of marriage as the avenue through which to deliver such support disadvantages real caregivers and those for whom they care. Removing the veil of marriage would increase the likelihood that benefits and protections aimed at caregiving units would serve their primary functions more effectively.

If we leave the definition and conferral of marital status to associations of civil society, do we not simply push marriage further back into the private sphere and invite radically illiberal versions of marriage such as polygamy to flourish?

This worry obscures important distinctions. Were marriage disestablished, some groups would openly sanction polygamous marriage. And if individuals from these groups both fit the socially determined but functionally defined prerequisites of a civil union aimed at protecting caregiving and took on that status, they would gain support and protection from the state. But they would receive support by virtue of their willingness to enter into the civil union, with its protection for caregiving activities, not by virtue of being married.[6] The state would still outlaw criminal behavior—say, spousal abuse or sex with a minor—and as feminists have long argued is necessary, criminal law would apply regardless of public label.[7]

In the end, our commitment to equality must be balanced by one to liberty. So, for instance, despite ample evidence that traditional marriage is bad for gender equality, few feminists call for the legal abolition of traditional marriage. Rather we advocate protections for those made vulnerable by the inequalities of such lifestyle choices. Underlying this concession are distinctions between public and private choices, actions and expressions. My proposal rests on these distinctions and, crucially, upon a clearer understanding of what makes marriage special. The separation I propose promises to benefit both marriage and the vulnerable.

Far from further obscuring injustice, then, disestablishing marriage and creating a civil-union status with particular attention to caregiving brings matters of concrete inequality and oppression to the fore.

Notes

1. Because of the inevitable, unpredictable, and diverse inequalities generated by intimate caregiving relationships, a state-administered regime of predetermined and legally enforced benefits and burdens, not a system of individual contracts, is best suited to the essential task of protecting such relationships.

2. I borrow the language of establishment from Nancy Cott's important book *Public Vows: A History of Marriage and the Nation*. She uses this language to describe an empirical trend. In my forthcoming Ph.D. dissertation, "Uneasy Union: Marriage and the State in Liberal Political Thought," I aim to provide a philosophical defense of the trend. By all forms of intimate caregiving unions, I mean same-sex couples and heterosexual couples, monogamous, open, polygamous, sexual, and nonsexual. The key is that these units would take on a legal status marking their members as primary mutual intimate caregivers. Shanley does not explicitly consider the alternative of such a status.

3. The growing numbers of heterosexual couples who, dissatisfied with both religious and state sanction, turn to trusted family members and friends to officiate at their weddings are but one example that supports this hypothesis. See "Need a Minister? How About Your Brother?" *New York Times*, Sunday, December 12, 2003.

4. We can and should distinguish between the meaning side of marriage—the social and normative accounts expressed by the word "marriage" that infuse the institution with social meaning—and the associated goods and relationships—divisible goods (money, property), practices (labor distribution), obligations, and children—with which the state is legitimately concerned.

5. I join Shanley in calling for greater social supports for families and the vulnerable more generally.

6. Metz, "Uneasy Union."

7. The example of marital rape is instructive here.

Mary Lyndon Shanley

Afterword

Since I wrote "Just Marriage," political and legal developments have accelerated and intensified the debate in a manner no one could have anticipated. As I write this reply in early March 2004, the Massachusetts Constitutional Convention is in recess and will reconvene shortly, having failed to pass a constitutional amendment defining marriage as a relationship between one man and one woman; the mayor of San Francisco has ordered city clerks to issue marriage licenses to same-sex couples, and attempts to stop them through the judicial system have so far failed; and the county clerk of Sandoval County, New Mexico, who began issuing marriage licenses to same-sex couples because she said she found nothing in the law to prevent it, has been ordered by the attorney general to stop. Not long ago the Ohio legislature passed a statute limiting marriage to heterosexual couples and barring state agencies from giving benefits to domestic partners of the same or opposite sex; courts in Arizona and New Jersey rejected various constitutional claims for the right of same-sex partners to marry.

These developments are clearly relevant to the discussion of justice and marriage that is the topic of this book, but the political debates over same-sex marriage differ in striking ways from the issues raised by the contributors here. In the public arena, defenses of the legal recognition of same-sex marriage like the majority opinion of the Massachusetts Supreme Judicial Court are grounded in a commitment to equal rights and nondiscrimination. Opposition to same-sex marriage, on the other hand, rests on traditional moral values, sometimes religious, and the right of the people (not the courts) to decide what marriage is and who may marry. Despite their differences, neither side questions whether marriage is a good thing and whether it should be recognized by the state; their argument is over who should be able to marry. But many of the contributors to this book go beyond these terms to raise basic questions about the meaning of marriage and its continuation as a civil institution.

Wendy Brown and Martha Fineman ask whether we should abolish marriage altogether or substitute some other institution in its place. Drucilla Cornell, Brenda Cossman, and Tamara Metz propose extending the benefits of state recognition to additional committed relationships such as single mothers or siblings living together or collective child-rearing households. Elizabeth Emens would include poly-

amorous relationships among these. Joan Tronto imagines
structures that would provide care for children outside of
nuclear families. William Eskridge, Amitai Etzioni, and Milton Regan Jr. want to retain marriage's civil status because
it helps people sustain personal commitments in the face of
what Brown calls the "unparalleled deracination" of contem-
porary life. Cass Sunstein points out both the uses and the
limitations of federalism as states seek to regulate marriage
in their own ways; and David Cruz argues that the liberal
state must remain neutral toward different people's understandings of the good life. Nancy Cott challenges us all to
identify the public purposes marriage may serve.

I remain committed to the main principles I espoused
in "Just Marriage"—the desirability of the state's recognition of committed adult relationships (as well as adult-child
relationships) and the state's promotion of equality between
marriage partners—but spurred by the intense public debate
of the past months, conversations with colleagues, and these
responses, my thinking about whether marriage as we know
it is the best form for this civil arrangement to take has
changed.[1]

I have come to realize that framing the issue as a choice
between "individual contract" and "public status" is inadequate. My aim was to reclaim the discussion of civil marriage from the grip of the far right and affirm the value of
public support for personal commitment. But the choice I
defined did not capture the range of possibilities. I rejected
individual contracts in lieu of marriage because they do not
account for the way in which commitment generates complex responsibilities that cannot be anticipated by individual

agreements. They also require financial resources beyond the reach of many and fail to acknowledge the public interest in supporting committed relationships. I proposed marriage as a civil institution—albeit a radically reconceived one—because civil status seemed to me to support the public dimension of marriage and thus provide the basis for insisting that the state support relationships of dependency and interdependency.

But as the essays in this volume make clear, there are numerous contenders for marriage's place as the state-sanctioned form of commitment, ranging from universal caregiving partnerships (Metz) to civil unions (Etzioni) to nonhorizontal intimate connections, particularly between parent and child (Fineman), to nonconjugal relationships of economic and emotional interdependency (Cossman) to polyamorous relationships (Emens) and more. My view now is that the United States should do away with the civil category of marriage and move to a legal regime of universal civil unions for heterosexual and homosexual couples alike, reserving the term "marriage" for unions sanctified by religious or other noncivil ceremonies. It was not "civil marriage" as distinct from "civil union" that I wished to defend (nor "civil union" as distinct from some other term), but rather the continuing relevance of giving civil status to committed and supportive adult relationships, including those that involve children.[2]

Using the term "civil union" also avoids the confusion generated by using the term "marriage" to refer both to a religious institution and to a civil one. United States law allows people to enter civil marriage through a religious ceremony. President Bush was not alone in insisting in the wake of *Goodridge v. Department of Public Health*, the Massachusetts same-sex marriage case, that the laws of the United States should defend "the sacred institution" of marriage. Yet a religiously pluralistic society that espouses the separation of church and state should not be protecting a "sacred" institution but a civil one. Both language and custom invite the conflation and confusion of the President's remark. Many countries, including Catholic France and Mexico, require a distinct civil ceremony, not just a church wedding, to establish a civil marriage. If we called the state-sanctioned institution "civil union," reserving the word "marriage" for unions sanctified by religious or other noncivil ceremonies, we could then think afresh about what we believe the public purposes of the state recognition of committed adult relationships to be.

The question that remains, as Nancy Cott says, is what public benefit today's society derives from retaining any state-sanctioned status for adult relationships.[3] One answer is that publicly recognizing ongoing relationships assigns them a symbolic value distinct from that of individualized contracts, which recognize the separateness of the contracting agents and the quid pro quo nature of their agreement. I agree with David Cruz that there is no need to invoke a marital "entity" to capture the relational aspect of human beings that is affirmed by their mutual commitment. This public affirmation of the couple's commitment is valuable to them; people attest that it is a source of psychological satisfaction, and it appears to enhance the durability of relationships. The social validation of committed relationships supports individuals' efforts to fulfill their responsibilities.

The state has an interest in making the lives of its citizens as secure as possible.

Another public purpose of civil unions is to protect the vulnerable. This is most obvious in the case of children. Children need committed caregivers who can provide emotional stability, psychological ties, and physical care, and the state should provide those caregivers with resources and hold them to their responsibilities. Civil unions are instruments that can be used to recognize and protect the complex relationships between children and the adults who care for them. As contributors to this volume point out, single motherhood, gay and lesbian parenting, collaborative procreation through the use of third-party eggs and sperm, blended families, and friendship groups have complicated the traditional understanding of who should be assigned the rights and responsibilities of a "parent." It is imperative that society, not individuals, establish the principles that govern parental rights and responsibilities.[4]

Adults who commit themselves to one another, like adults who assume responsibility for children, may face vulnerabilities that arise from their relationship—vulnerabilities that come from the commitment itself. All human beings can rightfully claim public support for shelter, sustenance, decent jobs, and health care. But it is not enough to give such benefits to individuals. A person in a committed relationship may need public recognition of that relationship to, say, request that an employer grant time off to allow him or her to care for a sick partner. Public recognition of the relational dimension of human life is significant not only for establishing eligibility for government benefits but also to enable people to make claims on the workplace and restructure it in ways that help them to sustain their significant commitments. And, as I argue in "Just Marriage," the economic and social structures that foster commitment must also promote both sexual and racial equality. Unless and until the context in which people enter into and fulfill their commitments is a just social order, just marriage will be elusive.

Even if there were agreement on these public purposes, the contributors here raise important questions to which neither they nor I have definitive answers. Brenda Cossman asks what criteria should be used to decide who is eligible for a civil union or a caregiving partnership and whether self-designation is sufficient. Elizabeth Emens and Drucilla Cornell raise, in different ways, questions about whether more than two adults might form a civil union and whether a sexual relationship must be an element of such a union. I ask in addition whether the law should grant some kind of limited parental status to an adult who is a child's nonprimary caregiver. David Cruz and Tamara Metz wonder how state recognition of relationships can avoid violating proper liberal neutrality concerning divergent conceptions of the good life.

The contributors to this volume work hard to make sense of what is happening in people's family lives, however constructed, and in legislatures, courts, and public debates. In doing so they join the struggle to shape a more just and humane future. Every response has made me think harder and, I hope, better. It should surprise no one that there is no consensus on how best to proceed and no final word in this book or in this ongoing discussion.

Notes

1. In particular, conversations with Matthew Kavanagh and Jo Ann Citron helped my thinking. Some of their ideas can be found in Matthew M. Kavanagh, "Re-Writing the Legal Family: Beyond Exclusivity to a Care-Based Standard," *Yale Journal of Law and Feminism* (spring 2004), and Jo Ann Citron, "Will It Be Marriage or Civil Union," *Gay and Lesbian Review Worldwide* 11, no. 2 (March–April 2004).

2. In their responses, Martha Fineman, Drucilla Cornell, and Tamara Metz object to my including Fineman among the proponents of contracts in lieu of marriage, pointing out that her primary concern has been to shift the focus of family law from the marital couple to the "mother/child dyad" (or, here, the nonhorizontal intimate connection), which is not a contractual relationship. That is true, and my advocacy of state support for that as well as other relationships is deeply indebted to Fineman's work and the ethic of care underlying it. But Fineman regards contracts as the appropriate tools for regulating relationships between adults unless one of them is in need of more-than-ordinary care. The tension between the understanding of humans as profoundly relational beings (the view that grounds discussions of parents and children) and the contrasting view of the autonomous adult related to others only through volition appears in differing views about both contractual and state regulation of family relationships throughout this volume and merits further attention.

3. In the past, among the purposes society attached to marriage were the transmission of property, the regulation of sexuality, and the legitimation of children. The rise of prenuptial agreements, the lack of prosecution for adultery or fornication, the end of the legal disabilities of nonmarital children, and other legal and social changes force us to think anew about the public purposes of marriage.

4. I address some of the ethical and legal issues concerning the grounding of parental rights and responsibilities in my book *Making Babies, Making Families: What Matters Most in an Age of Reproductive Technologies, Surrogacy, Adoption, and Same-Sex and Unwed Parents* (Beacon, 2001).